CABIN JOHN
Legends and Life of an Uncommon Place

Judith Welles

To those who know the real treasure of Cabin John.

Library of Congress control number: 2008903406

Published by the Cabin John Citizens Association, Cabin John, Maryland 20818

Printed by Signature Book Printing

For information or to order copies, write to P.O. Box 31, Cabin John, MD 20818 or
see *www.cabinjohn.org*

Cover photo: Photographer Alex J. Yowell built his studio under the Cabin John or Union Arch Bridge. Postcards of his pictures of the bridge in the early 1900s are found on eBay. Courtesy Richard Cook.

Contents

Foreword v

Chapter 1. Legends 1

Chapter 2. River, Canal, and Roads.................................... 9

Chapter 3. Rural to Residential... 22

Chapter 4. Union Arch Bridge.. 52

Chapter 5. Cabin John Bridge Hotel 65

Chapter 6. A Community Grows.. 79

Chapter 7. A Way of Life 113

Chapter 8. Epilogue.. 126

Locktenders 128
Citizen Association Presidents 129
Fire Chiefs 130
The Village News Editors 131

Bibliography... 132
Illustrations... 135
Index.. 139
About the Author... 144

Foreword

Who or what is Cabin John? The name Cabin John is steeped in mystery and legend. But Cabin John is much more than a legend.

Cabin John, a community in Maryland, has historical significance. If you lived near the turn of the century, 1900, you bought two-cent postcards of the scenic Union Arch Bridge (a.k.a. Cabin John Bridge) or photographs of the Cabin John Bridge Hotel. With these sights, Cabin John was a retreat destination for Washington residents and a major attraction for tourists. Today, postcards of the engineering marvel of the bridge or photographs of the architectural whimsy of the hotel command more than a hundredfold increase in value on eBay.

The bridge, once the longest single-span stone arch in the world and still the longest in the United States, carries the aqueduct that gave Washington, D.C., its first public water. John Philip Sousa introduced his famous "Washington Post March" on a bandstand in the hotel's expansive gardens. Several U.S. Presidents dined in the hotel restaurant.

Cabin John also has architectural significance. Some of the original mail-order Sears kit houses still stand from the 1920s. Other architecturally interesting houses include one with compressed dirt walls, another built of logs, and even a Tuscan-style villa.

Beside the Potomac River and the Chesapeake and Ohio Canal National Historical Park, Cabin John has amazing natural diversity. Birds and flora rarely seen in one location anywhere in the Mid-Atlantic states abound.

Maybe it's the river, maybe it's the light, and maybe it's the live-and-let-live feeling of the small community that has attracted artists, writers and musicians. They live among lawyers, doctors and scientists, and next door to plumbers, carpenters and small shop owners.

Former Vice President Hubert Humphrey's political career had its origin in Cabin John. Former Montgomery County Executive Neal Potter grew up in Cabin John. Dr. George Weil, who with Enrico Fermi started the first sustained nuclear chain reaction, lived

v

in Cabin John. In the distant past, Irish workmen, lockkeepers and boatmen of the C&O Canal lived in Cabin John next to dairy, corn and grain farmers.

For those who live here, Cabin John is a state of mind. For others, Cabin John is a place in Maryland, close to Washington, D.C. For all who know Cabin John, and for those who will come to know it, this book gives a glimpse of the past and the present of a community imbued with character and charm.

My thanks to Andrew Rice, resident historian, editor and writer, who encouraged me and whose insight and articles in Cabin John's *The Village News* informed me. My sincere appreciation to the Cabin John Citizens Association which supported the book project and to Burton "Burr" Gray, president, for inspiring it.

My gratitude also to Montgomery County. This publication has been financed in part by Montgomery County Historic Preservation Commission funds which are administered by the Historic Preservation Section of the Montgomery County Department of Park and Planning.

The book began with a meeting at Andy's house with Burr, Reed and Barbara Martin, my husband Tim Shank and me on a Sunday afternoon, February 18, 2007. Subsequently, other Cabin John residents and collectors of Cabin John memorabilia and history, including Richard Cook, Richard Hirsh and Carlotta Anderson opened their own collections of documents and photos.

Trudy Nicholson helped with research and proofing as did Reed and Barbara Martin. *The Village News* editors Mike Miller's and Tim Weedlun's effort to digitize the complete archives of newsletters had the side benefit of aiding this book. I am grateful to Tim Weedlun who applied his graphic artistry to design this book for publication.

Edith M. Armstrong and Elizabeth Kytle deserve much credit for their early histories, *Brief History of Cabin John Park* and *Time Was*, respectively, which provided flavor and context for this book. Many present and former Cabin John residents gave me their photos and memories of the 1940s, '50s and '60s to the present, including Uva Cable, Christine Gates Cerniglia, Kathleen Gates Carroll, Tommy and Naomi Denell, Dawn Fyock, Elaine Hornauer, Dana Lupton, Evan Mater, Forrest and Lorraine Minor, Mary Hook Morgal, David Murphy, Olivia Murphy, Gerald Quinn, Marion Sullivan, Wayne Swisher, and Maureen Willoughby.

Finally, my husband provided not only rigorous research, copyediting, indexing and photography but the patience and understanding that allowed me to write this book.

Collecting and weaving together the facts and lore of Cabin John has been a fascinating journey. Many deserve credit for the details they provided, but any errors are mine alone. Even though the memories were of times past, the present is not so much different, with many of the same qualities and issues still characteristic of Cabin John life.

— *Judy Welles*
June 2008

Courtesy Richard Cook

Canoeing on the Potomac River from Cabin John was a favorite pastime in 1900 just as today.

Timeline

1608 Captain John Smith's voyage on the Potomac River.

1688 Early mention of a Captain John's Creek by Maryland Assembly.

1715 Captain John's Run, also known as Captain John's Creek, identified as property line in Fletchall's Garden land record.

1742 Maryland legislature pays 300 pounds to Indians for land.

1830 C&O Canal construction reaches Cabin John; locktender's house at Lock 8 built for $750; locks 8-14 become known as the Seven Locks.

1850 C&O Canal operations begin; Irish workers on the canal settle in area of Cabin John.

1857 Cabin John (Union Arch) Bridge construction begins; bridge carries Washington Aqueduct bringing water to the District of Columbia.

1864 Union troops protect the bridge and canal during Civil War; Jefferson Davis name is removed from the Bridge.

1867 Land for first school for white children purchased for $5 on what would later be Persimmon Tree Road.

1870 Bobingers build Cabin John Bridge Hotel.

1874 Hermon Presbyterian Church, first church for Cabin John, established by congregants from Captain John's Meeting House in Potomac.

1880 Moore's School established, first school for African American children in Cabin John.

1884 First school for white children, built of logs, replaced by a one-room frame building named Friendship School on Persimmon Tree Road.

1885 Ten African American families purchase lots and build homes on Number 10 Road, later renamed Seven Locks Road.

1889 Major flood seriously damages C&O Canal.

1898 Gibson Grove AME Zion Church built.

1909 Jefferson Davis' name restored to Union Arch Bridge.

1912 American Land Company begins sales of Cabin John Park homesites.

1919 Cabin John Park Citizens Association founded.

1920s Electricity comes to homes; Home Demonstration Club founded; first Sears houses built in Cabin John.

1921 G. W. Shaler Memorial Methodist Episcopal Church of Cabin John established.

1924 C&O Canal operations end following major flood.

1928 Glen Echo-Cabin John School opens in Cabin John; name changed to Clara Barton School in 1944.

1930 Cabin John Firehouse built; sold in 1984.

1931 Cabin John Bridge Hotel burns down.

1936 Massive flooding of Potomac River sends residents from homes to safety in firehouse.

1938 U.S. Department of Interior buys C&O Canal property.

1942 Cabin John Gardens and Carver Road homes built for federal workers at David Taylor Model Basin.

1954 Clara Barton becomes one of the first schools in Montgomery County to integrate.

Supreme Court Justice William Douglas walks the 184.5 miles of the C&O Canal to support preserving it.

1963   Clara Barton Parkway opens.

1967   *The Village News* begins publication.

1970   Community Plan developed; annual Crab Feast begins.

1972   C&O Canal becomes a national historical park.

1974   700-pound section falls from ledge of Cabin John
        Bridge to parkway below, closing bridge for repair for
        more than one year.

1976   Cabin John Bridge reopens with civic and
        political celebration.

1980   MacArthur Plaza shopping center built.

1983   Bethesda Co-Op moves to Cabin John.

1998   Photographic history display installed at Cabin John
        Post Office.

2000   Cabin John goes online with Citizen Association
        Web site; history panels developed for display in Clara
        Barton Community Center.

2008   Community celebrates 400th Anniversary of Captain
        John Smith's voyage to the vicinity of Cabin John.

Chapter 1
Legends

The mystery surrounding the name Cabin John has led to many stories about pirates, ghosts, lost lovers, and more.

The Hermit

One story tells of a hermit named John who lived in a cabin next to the creek where the aqueduct Union Arch Bridge was later built. This reclusive man stayed away from neighbors and when asked his name replied, "Call me John." He dressed in raccoon skins, had a pack of dogs, and appeared to be a hunter with a rifle who lived on fish and game.

The story was also reported in *The Washington Star* newspaper in 1913. It said that a poem was found in 1825 in a grain bin in an old mill on the banks of Cabin John Creek:

> *"John of the Cabin – a curious wight*
> *Sprang out of the river one dark stormy night:*
> *He built a warm hut in a lonely retreat,*
> *And lived many years on fishes and meat.*
> *When the last lone raccoon on the creek he had slain,*
> *It is said he jumped into the river again.*
> *As no name to the creek by the ancients was given,*
> *It was called 'Cabin John' after John went to Heaven."*

In 1903, J. H. Wilson Marriott, author of *Picturesque Cabin John: A Bit of History*, wrote of meeting an elderly gentleman on River Road who told what his father had told him. The story was that in 1790, an Indian appeared and erected his cabin by the creek that later bore his name "John." To further substantiate the story, the man recalled that as a boy he had frequently found arrow, spear, and axe heads in and around the old cabin.

The Lovers

In another version, the hermit was the husband of the "female stranger" whose tombstone is in Alexandria, Virginia. She may have been a nobleman's daughter in England pledged to marry royalty before she fled with her lover to America. A variation insists that John killed a man in a fight over the woman and the couple then fled England. After arriving in America, the couple would not reveal their names out of fear of being punished for the crime.

The *Boston Herald Traveler* in 1971 wrote of a couple named John and Ellen Trust who had fled England and arrived at Gadsby's Tavern in Alexandria. On route to America, Ellen became ill with ship fever and died shortly after arriving in 1816. John, fearing reprisal, buried her with the words "female stranger" and no name on her tombstone. The tombstone reads, "To the memory of a female stranger whose mortal sufferings terminated on the 14th day of October 1816, aged 23 years and 8 months. This stone is placed here by her disconsolate husband in whose arms she sighed out her latest breath and who under God did his utmost even to soothe the cold dead ear of death."

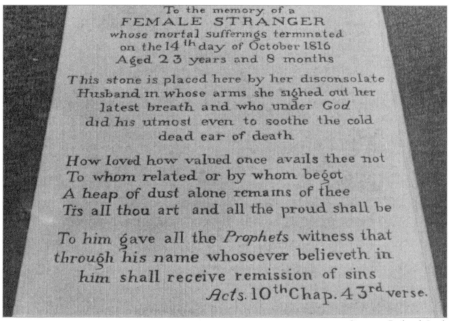

Courtesy Richard Cook

The gravestone depicted in a book confirmed the legend of the female stranger.

In this story, John then drifted north into Maryland and spent time doing odd jobs, hunting and fishing. By 1845, he became well known as "Cabin John." He built a small boat and traveled down the Potomac River to visit his wife's grave. But by 1851, too old to row down the river, he wrote to his brother Harold, asking him to come from England to America for a final meeting. When Harold Trust reached his brother's shack, he found this note:

Dear Brother – I have waited for you but now it is too late. Bury me with her in the Cemetery in Alexandria. Her grave is marked FEMALE STRANGER. Take me there at night. John

Harold found the bones of his brother with a family ring beside a creek. He had the cabin destroyed and in the dark of night, men rowed silently to Alexandria. They placed the mortal remains of John Trust beside his long dead wife.

In 1912, a romance novel, *The Legend of the "Female Stranger,"* A *Tale of Cabin John Bridge and Old Alexandria*, was widely circulated with the story which added to the attraction of Cabin John Bridge Hotel.

In 1939, another version of the female stranger story appeared, this one by Elizabeth Hannen, a Cabin John resident whose husband had been president of the Cabin John Park Citizens Association. She wrote that just after the Revolutionary War, there was a beautiful English noblewoman who was an orphan and the ward of an elderly gentleman. He became fond of her and wanted to marry her but she loved a man named John Smith who was not of nobility. When her guardian found out, he and John came to blows. In the fight, John accidentally killed the guardian. So under cover of darkness John and his bride left on a ship captained by his brother who, with the crew, helped build the cabin for them.

When published in 1912, a book on the legend of the female stranger aroused romantic images about Cabin John.

Courtesy Richard Cook

The Pirate

On August 9, 1896, a *Washington Post* article identified John of the Cabin as a pirate from Jamaica because he "amused himself by playing upon a little instrument made by his own hands and said to resemble a banjo." The writer concluded that he must have been acquainted with the West Indies "since the banjo was then in the early stages of its evolution." Adding to the story, a man named John Cecil, a planter from Jamaica, had married a beautiful young widow in South Carolina but left her to gain wealth through piracy. The report continued that after many years had passed, about the time of the disappearance of John of the Cabin, an old man appeared at a plantation asking for Mrs. Cecil. When told she had died, the man wept, and the next day was found floating in a river.

A *Washington Star* article on April 6, 1913, attributed a detailed description of John of the Cabin's physical appearance and habits to "the citizens of that community who got their information from their fathers, grandfathers and great-grandfathers." According to the article, "He made his own clothes, and they were heavy and flowing garments of skins of wild animals caught or killed in the neighborhood. Because of these garments he had quite the appearance of a woman when some distance away. He avoided all kinds of companionship, but was never known to do an unkind or harmful act...

"At times curious persons ventured in the vicinity of the cabin and frequently they would hear music on some peculiar instrument, and sometimes he would sing songs and quaint and touching melodies in a foreign language..."

The article also determined that John's past must have included ship life since tattoos were observed covering his arms, legs, and entire body. "This information was obtained from some boys who stole through the bushes until they were very near John one summer day while bathing in the creek....Had he been simply a Maryland farm boy he doubtless would not have been thus decorated."

Edith M. Armstrong wrote in her *Brief History of Cabin John Park*, "Another story makes the mysterious John a pirate who eluded his own crew and made his way up the Potomac to bury his treasure." The American Land Company that sold lots for

A drawing of the hermit's cabin appeared in a book Picturesque Cabin John: A Bit of History, *published in 1903.*

Courtesy Richard Cook

Cabin John Park housing in 1912 trusted that story enough, or saw its marketing potential, to write a provision into property deeds that

"The Party of the first part reserves the right to one-half interest in any treasure or articles of special value which may have been hidden on said lot or parcel by John of the Cabin."

Armstrong wrote that after John of the Cabin had disappeared, and perhaps had died, he was said to return when the wind was strong with a rifle on his shoulder but, when sighted, would disappear into a flare of light. She wrote that because some believed this version, "...for a long time, they would never cross the bridge after midnight, especially on a Saturday."

Some photographs in the late 1800s of the Cabin John/Union Arch Bridge show a small cabin just below the arch. The Montgomery County Historical Society described correspondence with the great-grandson of Montgomery Meigs, Roy C. Smith, a retired Naval officer living in Annapolis, who told the story his mother told him: "When

Courtesy Richard Cook

A cabin for workmen located under the Union Arch Bridge, ca. 1880, may have led to legends.

he [Meigs] built the aqueduct, the Cabin John Bridge...there was an old slave named John, an escaped slave who went into the wild country there and gathered together pieces of wood and he made this cabin. I remember it very well, right on the edge of the water. Rock Creek (sic) then was a lovely limpid stream and there was the water running by and he lived there and in the design for the aqueduct the arch of the bridge sprung right over his little hut. Grandfather turned everybody else off the government reservation but he left old John to live there in peace..."

The Real Story?

The fascination with John of the Cabin continued for years. However, long before the stories of lovers and pirates, court and land records include references to a Captain John's Run or Branch, now Cabin John Creek. A land record for Fletchall's Garden in 1715 described the property bordered by Captain John's Run. Indeed, the first church, Captain John's Meeting House, was built in 1716 in Potomac, Maryland, an area labeled "Captain John's Section" on colonial maps. Perhaps Cabin John is a corrupt spelling of Captain John. But who was Captain John?

There was a Captain John Moore who owned stone quarries in the area after 1812 but that would have been nearly 100 years later than documents that name the creek. More likely, Captain John was Captain John Smith, one of the founders of Jamestown and the first man to map the Potomac River. He traveled by boat as far as Little Falls, a few miles down river, and by land to the mouth of what became Captain John's/Cabin John Creek and through the area of Cabin John to Great Falls. His journal described his voyage of exploration up the Potowomack River from the Chesapeake Bay during June 18 to July 15, 1608:

"The river...maketh his passage downe a low pleasant valley overshadowed in manie places with high rocky mountain from whence distill innumerable sweet and pleasant springs...Having gone so high as we could with the bote we met divers salvages in canowes well loaden with flesh of beares, deere, and other beasts wherof we had part. Here we found mighty rocks growing in some places above the ground as high as the shrubby tree...Digging the growne above in the highest clifts of rocks we saw it was a claie sand so mixed with yellow spangles as if it had been half pin-dust."

In her book *Potomac Adventure*, Ann Patterson Harris wrote that it is quite possible that during the 17th century colonists referred to traveling the river as far as had Captain John. Afterall, it was in the area of the mouth of the stream later called Cabin John Creek that Smith stopped to trade with the Indians.

In a book published in 1931, *Tidewater Maryland*, is found this reference: "By 1688 the Maryland Assembly had ordered the building of 62 towns, and the sites for them were named. These sites were all on navigable waters, and generally at the end of the tide's reach inland, or where the running, fresh-water rivers began to be navigable....Among the localities where towns were ordered were...at Captain John's Creek." While there may have been another Captain John's Creek in Maryland, the fact remains that Captain John Smith's river travels led to the naming of creeks after him.

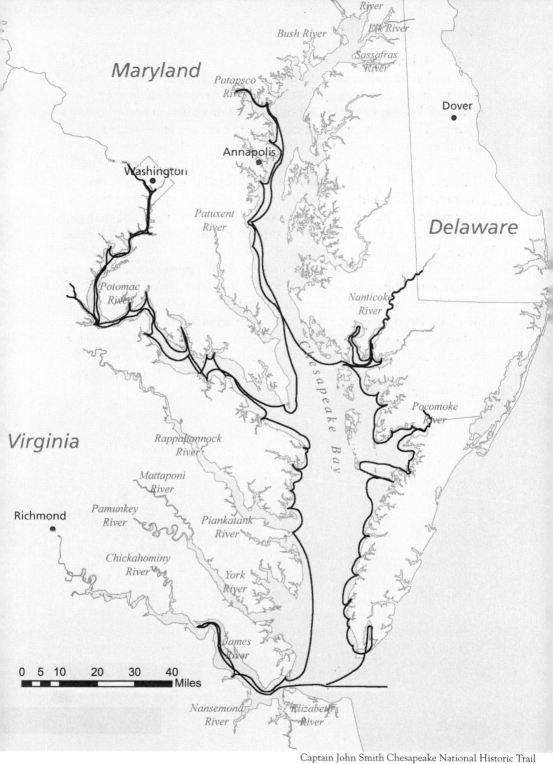

Captain John Smith Chesapeake National Historic Trail

Captain John Smith's journeys June 2 - July 21, 1608 along the Potomac River from the Chesapeake Bay came through the area that became Cabin John.

By 1803, the name Cabin John appeared as Cabin John Mills, a flour and grain mill. An item in the August 8, 1821 issue of the *Daily National Intelligencer* newspaper stated, "For rent valuable merchant mills well known by the name of Cabin John Mills in Montgomery County. These mills are on a never-failing stream and are capable of manufacturing from 40 to 50 barrels of flour a day...."

The mystery and legends of Cabin John gave the community distinction in 1984. General Motors selected Cabin John as one of six communities with names of such interesting origin that they were featured in its full color 75-page book on the new Buick of that year. Included were photos of the "Cabin John Park Vol. Fire Dept." and several homes.

Indeed, there may have been a hermit-like person or freed slave or someone needing a place to live who built a shack-like cabin at various times near Cabin John Creek in the valley below the bridge. There may have been people named John. But whether that led to the name Cabin John may have come more from the storyteller than the real story. In 2008 the community of Cabin John celebrated the 400th anniversary of Captain John Smith's voyage on the Potomac River. And the legends live on.

Chapter 2
River, Canal, and Roads

Location, location, for Cabin John, it is all about location. Today, Cabin John is minutes from the nation's capital by several roads, traveling routes used for more than 200 years. It is also an access point to the modern-day beltway that circles Washington, D.C., and leads to major highways to northern and southern states. Northwest of Washington, on the Potomac River and C&O Canal, Cabin John is eight miles northwest of Georgetown and six miles southeast of Great Falls, Maryland.

Early maps of the area show the importance of waterways, with markings for the Potomac River, Captain John's Run or Branch and later Cabin John Creek, and in the mid-1800s the C&O Canal. These waters were used for transporting goods, fishing, sightseeing, and in the case of Cabin John Creek, powering Cabin John Mills.

Potomac River

The Potomac River is an important part of Cabin John. Not only did the river bring Captain John Smith "so high as we could bote," but some 68 different spellings of Potomac in Indian terms, such as Potowomack, tell a story of a "river full of swarms of small fry" or "when fishes spawn," or "traveling traders."

The McMillan Commission, which produced the 1902 plan for developing the Federal City of Washington, D.C., declared: "The best scenery lies beyond [the District Line], especially in the neighborhood of Cabin John Creek and in the region just above and below Great Falls."

As Edith Armstrong wrote in 1947 and still true today, "No one can deny that the rugged shoreline, rapids, and islands create a beauty that is superb. The abundance of wild flowers and birds along the banks has long been a joy to all." Cabin John is a destination for lovers of nature and the outdoors.

ROCKVILLE DIST.
Nº 4.
Mont. Co.
Scale 2 Inches to the Mile.

WATKINS I.D.

DA

Sandy B

Bell's Old Mill

John Gt

Susan Green

Susan L
R.C. Cream

Occup

Jno. Creamer

Martha Myers

Wm T. Fisher

Sam¹ Jo

Gris. Mill

Wm Dooley

Elbert Perry

G. McCormich

RIVER

Grimes Lock

Jno. P. Connell
Res.

Wm G Connell
Res.

Great Falls of the Potomac

Falls I.d.

Conn I.d.

CANAL

OHIO

H. A. Garrett

Mont. Clagett

D. Clagett

H. Garrett

B.S.Sh.
Store
Garrett Gate House
Water Works
Hotel

Capt Jno. McDonald

Curry

Robt. G. Connell
Res.

Garrett
& Maus

Sam¹ Ford

Dr. J. W. Anderson
Hrs.

Great Falls
Ice Ho.

Gold
Mine

L. Mortimer Offutt

Club Ho.

Ann Connell, Hrs.

Offutts X Roads P.O.

Falls

J. H. Welsh

Sch. Ho.

Potomac
M. E. Ch.
South

H. Garrett

Martha Meye

B.S.Sh.
T. E. Perry

Dr. C. F. Willett

Josiah

Wm Offutt

L. E. Collins

P. Houser
J. Burriss

J. W. Carroll
Res.

Sch. Ho.

J. W. Collins

Wm Hardesty

Wm Collins

Wm Clagett

Henry Haines

Jno. Hinton

Jos. J. Stearn
Res.

Thos W Offutt

Run

H. C. Fausett
Res.

Harriett Stone

Robt. G. Davidson

Geo. G. Bradley

Henry Bradley

Henry Br
Res.

Rock

Philip Stone, Hrs.

Mrs. Offutt

Judge Casey

Wm S. Harrison

Richd Cropley
Jno. W. Radcliff
Jno. Stone

Mrs. M. Carter

Jno. G. Stone

Josh. W. Offutt
Res.

Jas. Ginger

Jno. Offutt

Richd Cropley

John Saunders
Res.

Henry Harding

Wm Everly

Jno. G. Trundle
Res.

Leghor

Seven

Dd. Lo
Occu
Dr. M.

E. Pickerell
Hrs.

Geo. Hill

Herman
Pres. Ch.
Dr. Offutt

Peter Jones

Thos Dowling

Old Paper
Mill

J. D. W. Moore

Res.
Spencer C. Jones
& Wm Brewer

Sylvester C. Jones
Res.

Res.
Jno. D. W. Moore

B. Hamilton

H. H. Chick
Occup

Ed. Magruder

Tho

Seven Locks

Friendship
Sch. Ho.

Harvey Shepperd
Josh W Offutt

BETHESDA

CHESAPEAKE

AND

OHIO

Canal

T. Bihee

Cabin John

Creek

T. Dobbings

Cabin John
Arch Bridge

tered according to Act of Congress in the year 1878 by G. M. Hopkins, in the Office of the Librarian of

VIRGINIA

Plummers Island is a small, 12-acre wooded island in the Potomac River accessible from a strip of land between Locks 10 and 12 of the C&O Canal. Known as the most thoroughly studied island in North America, the island has been home to the Washington Biologists Field Club since 1901. The biologists club purchased the island in 1908, along with 38 acres of the buffer land between it and the canal, and built a small wooden house on the highest rocky point. Major floods have scoured the island over the years and renewed the flora to more than 885 species.

Loretta Tuohey Hall, granddaughter of one of the earliest Cabin John residents, recalled childhood memories of the river. "You've walked across that river because it's been so low. You've skated across it. And you've nearly drowned in it."

The river has a record of floods that threatened people and caused extensive damage to their property and to the C&O Canal. The most devastating floods were in 1889, 1924, and 1936. On April 17, 1936, a flood drove people from homes close to the canal to seek shelter at the Cabin John firehouse. Jack Fields and his sister Lillian remembered as youngsters watching the river reach the second floor of the lockhouse at Lock 8 as the water came halfway up the hill toward the house where they lived.

Birdie Hook, shown with Lee Wallace in 1920, saw the flood from the end of Woodrow Avenue (79th Street).

Courtesy Mary Hook Morgal

Mary Hook Morgal said, "I remember the flood of '36 and my grandmother [Birdie Hook] took us across to sit on the bank and look at the water and it was running through the top window of the lockhouse."

Another historic flood occurred in June, 1972, following Hurricane Agnes. Larry Heflin took his canoe into the river which had risen above the canal behind his Riverside Drive house. "I paddled past the roof of the lockhouse [at Lock 8] before wrapping the canoe around a treetop in the river behind Glen Echo Park," he recounted.

Opposite: G. M. Hopkins' 1878 map shows Conduit Road, the Seven Locks, Cabin John Creek, Union Arch Bridge, Bobinger's Hotel, and Thomas Tuohey's ("T. Tuhee") home.

Courtesy Elaine Hornauer

Left: *Cabin John residents saw the Potomac River reach historic flood levels in 1936, engulfing Lockhouse 8.*

Below: *In 1938, Civilian Conservation Corps photographers documented the 1936 flood's damage to Lock 8.*

Courtesy Christine
Gates Cerniglia

National Park Service

C&O Canal

The Potomac River, with a rocky bed and falls, is unnavigable above Little Falls. The construction of the C&O Canal, beginning in 1828, was designed to provide a more navigable waterway to open trade and transport to the West. The idea came from the Potowmack Company, incorporated in 1784, in which George Washington was a principal investor. That company constructed a few locks on the Virginia side of the Potomac River but failed by 1819. With the success of the Erie Canal in New York State, another attempt seemed possible and the Chesapeake & Ohio Canal Company was formed with federal and state aid.

Cabin John and the canal are linked in history. On March 18, 1829, the C&O Canal Company received a proposal from James O'Brien for erecting house "Numbers 5 and 6" at a cost of $725 each.

Number 5 is the lockhouse at Lock 7 in Glen Echo and Number 6 is the stone house at Lock 8 in Cabin John.

In 1830, the lockhouse at Lock 10 was built with similar design by a different contractor, H.W. Maynard, also at a cost of $725. The lockhouses were ready for occupancy by locktenders in the summer of 1830.

Montgomery County Historical Society

The locktender helps a C&O Canal Company payboat through Lock 8 in 1910.

Lock 8 is the first of the series of locks known as 'Seven Locks' – Locks 8, 9, 10, 11, 12, 13 and 14 – which raise the C&O Canal 56 feet over the distance of one and a quarter mile. These are the locks that gave the name to Seven Locks Road.

Just above Lock 8, the canal is 100 feet wide, once providing a turning basin for the canal boats coming downstream from Cumberland and meeting other boats coming upstream from Georgetown. Today it is a place frequented by great blue and green herons, woodpeckers, ducks and many other birds. The Potomac River can be seen through a narrow buffer of trees.

Remarkably, despite financial and physical obstacles, the C&O Canal Company completed the first 17 mile stretch of the canal to Seneca Creek by 1831. Indentured Irish laborers encountered many problems with rival factions of workers and outbreaks of cholera. Graves dotted the canal between Cabin John and Great Falls.

The canal played a key role in the early history of Cabin John. The canal brought livelihood for its builders, locktenders and boatmen,

National Park Service

Lockhouse 8, built in 1830, as it appeared in 1938, with houses on the hill behind it.

and products, such as flour and stone, for the developing community where later many of them lived.

The canal was also annoying to the new community because the loud horn or the call of "He-ey Lock" awoke many residents at night when it failed to wake the locktender. With the canal just down the hill from their homes, residents could see lights from swinging lanterns, and hear the bells on the mules pulling the boats along the canal and the water rushing to fill or empty the lock. During the day,

J. S. Tomlinson brochure; courtesy Richard Cook

Lock 9 "waithouse" used by locktenders in inclement weather and Lockhouse 10, beyond, in 1913.

National Park Service

Lockhouse 9, damaged by floods and later a squatters house, was dismantled by the Park Service ca. 1939.

they watched the boats pass slowly along, many with families with their small children tied to the decks to keep them from falling into the canal.

By 1924, floods and the railroad put the C&O Canal Company in bankruptcy, and canal operations stopped. For several years, pleasure boats came occasionally through locks near Georgetown and Cabin John. The U.S. Department of the Interior bought the canal and adjacent land from the Chesapeake and Ohio Railroad for $2 million in 1938 amid growing interest in paving over the canal for a better road.

But, in 1954, after Supreme Court Justice William O. Douglas hiked from Cumberland, Md., to Georgetown in Washington, D.C. – the entire 184.5 mile length – with supporters and reporters, new attention focused on the outdoor attraction, natural diversity and historical importance of the C&O Canal. Plummers Island and its mainland acreage passed to the National Park Service in

Tim Shank

In 2000, Lockhouse 10 was occupied and renovated by residents under a stewardship agreement with the National Park Service.

1959. Finally, in 1971, the C&O Canal became the nation's longest, narrowest national park, accessible in many locations including Cabin John. Residents and thousands of park visitors are seen walking, jogging, biking along the towpath every day.

Tim Weedlun

Joggers, cyclists, and casual strollers make frequent use of the towpath today.

Roads

Until about 1850, roads in the area were barely passable, and poor transportation made it difficult to move crops to market. The earliest roads in Montgomery County can be seen on Dennis Griffith's 1794 map, which shows a major route from Georgetown that later became River Road. This road marked the northern boundary of what became Cabin John.

River Road, once an Indian trail, remained a dirt road until the mid-1800s. The only access to Cabin John from River Road was Number 10 Road, which was renamed Seven Locks Road when Montgomery County revised road names in the 1950s. According to William Offutt, Number 10 was named for the ten houses built by black families who worked on the farm and quarry owned by John Moore. He sold the lots to them for low prices.

Seven Locks, the original name for Persimmon Tree Road, was laid out in 1869. It was a narrow dirt road that ended at Lock 10 on the C&O Canal, the middle of the Seven Locks section of the canal. It was later renamed State Road and then Persimmon Tree Road because of the many tall persimmon trees found along the road.

Conduit Road, named for the aqueduct beneath it and renamed MacArthur Boulevard for Gen. Douglas MacArthur by an act of Congress during World War II, was never intended for transportation. The road was actually the cover of a brick-lined tunnel built by the U.S. Corps of Engineers to bring a water supply from Great Falls to Washington, D.C. The conduit crossed Cabin John Creek through the Union Arch Bridge. The road curved left and right as it passed out of Cabin John to Washington as a result of the contour of the land and also because the aqueduct was designed with angles to slow the flow of water.

When the conduit was completed in 1863, area farmers began to use the smooth clay surface as a roadway. Between 1870 and 1875, a

$46,000 appropriation allowed the road to have a macadam topping for about a mile. Some saw the change as a more efficient way for bringing farm products to market.

Explaining why farmers used Conduit Road instead of River Road, Norman Tuohey recalled, "Because it was the only flat place

J. S. Tomlinson brochure; courtesy Richard Cook

A view of Conduit Road, Cabin John's main street, in 1912.

around, people – farmers with their wagons – started driving on it. Something had to be done to protect the conduit, so the government engineers finally put this stone base down or else the wagons would have cut though. River Road was only wide enough for one horse and wagon and if you met somebody you'd have a heck of a time."

While a road may have been needed for farm wagons to bring produce to Washington, D.C., there was a different reason for building a road on the conduit. The U.S. Corps of Engineers' *History of the Washington Aqueduct* pointed out that a road was necessary between Cabin John and Great Falls to bring equipment for maintenance and repair of the conduit. When heavier trucks carrying coal and oil started using the road, the need for weight limits became necessary to protect the conduit.

Tim Shank

MacArthur Boulevard, covering the conduit for the Washington Aqueduct, has truck weight restrictions.

17

Paved of Gold?

There had been a gold mine within a few miles of Cabin John and during the Civil War, soldiers observed the gold dust glitter on Conduit Road and made promises to themselves to return to make their fortunes in the future.

In fact, the road was macadamized in the 1870s with gold-bearing quartz and much of it assayed as high as $16 a ton at that time, according to a report by the Institute of Mining Engineers in 1890.

A *Washington Post* article of February 3, 1913, included the commentary that most people of the time did not know that "perhaps the Conduit Road leading to Cabin John Bridge and Great Falls is literally paved with gold. But it's a fact. ..Some years ago there was considerable excitement among mining engineers over the discovery near Great Falls of gold ore...The dumpings from some of these mines were used to repair the Conduit Road, and for many years afterwards, when it rained small pieces of gold could be picked up on that road."

Even today, families and children have panned minute particles of gold from Cabin John Creek.

Several Presidents were known to travel Conduit Road to the Union Arch Bridge and to Great Falls. Abraham Lincoln inspected the progress on the bridge. Grover Cleveland drove to the bridge in 1885. Theodore Roosevelt enjoyed chauffeur-driven rides to and across the bridge through Cabin John to Great Falls.

In 1905, the *Washington Post* reported that President Roosevelt's car had been pursued near Cabin John by two policemen on bicycles. The chauffeur thought they were helping to clear the way until one of the policemen demanded that the automobile stop.

"What is the problem..." asked the passenger from the rear of the car.

"You have violated the speed regulation," said the policeman, "you were going at least twenty-five miles an hour and the regulation allows but fifteen." When informed that he was addressing the President, the officer collapsed and the second policeman "hastily carried him to the rear." The report continued that the President took the matter good-naturedly and, after crossing the bridge, instructed the chauffeur to proceed at a more moderate rate of speed.

Conduit Road also became the favorite drive of President Woodrow Wilson and Mrs. Wilson in the middle of the afternoon. Mrs. Josephine Havens, an early resident, recalled seeing them numerous times in a long, black, chauffeur-driven car which looked like a Pierce Arrow. "I gathered it must have been one of his favorite drives. He used to ride out to Great Falls. You didn't see too many people going by in cars, so when I'd see him I'd always wave. He didn't wave back, but I'd get a nod. Sometimes he'd be alone...and sometimes Mrs. Wilson was with him."

During the 1920s, those who drove by car into Washington had to obtain a District of Columbia license as well as a Maryland one and vice versa. Because the road was government property, the people of Washington could drive on it without securing a Maryland tag provided they did not leave the road. "This resulted in frequent controversies with people who had misjudged the width of the Government property," Armstrong wrote in her 1947 history.

The Potomac River marks the southern boundary of Cabin John. MacArthur Boulevard parallels the river as does the Clara Barton Parkway, originally the George Washington Parkway on the Maryland side that was built in the 1960s.

Today, Persimmon Tree Road is the western boundary of the community but early Cabin John extended beyond Persimmon Tree/Seven Locks Road. It included the Potter farm and the dirt road, later called Navy Truck Road and, even later, Eggert, until postal boundaries were reset.

The land for the Cohassett Road, on the east side of Cabin John Creek, was purchased in 1878 and the name changed to Wilson Lane in 1928 because the lane once led to a farm owned by a family named Wilson.

Along with improved roads came the development of stage lines and trolleys. Passenger use increased with tourism in the late 1800s to early 1900s. Excitement over the engineering marvel of a stone arch bridge, scenic vistas unparalleled in the region, and an ornate Victorian hotel with steel walkways over gorges and amusements drew crowds. Excursions brought visitors by canal boats, organized walks, horse and buggy, and even bicycles. In June 1889, the *Washington Post* reported that a travel time of 38 minutes by bicycle from 9th & G streets in Washington to Cabin John, a distance of ten miles, broke the record set in 1887.

In 1896, the Washington and Great Falls Electrical Railway ran from Georgetown along the Potomac River to Glen Echo and Cabin John. The open-air cars gave passengers expansive and breathtaking views of the river on trips during the summer. The trolley ran until 1960.

Today, the only public transportation in and out of Cabin John is on Montgomery County's small ride-on buses that take passengers to major bus and metro subway hubs in Bethesda during rush hours.

Highways

A major road, the Washington beltway or Interstate 495, was completed in 1964. It originally included plans to cross the Potomac River close to the end of Seven Locks Road, a design that would have obliterated Cabin John from the map entirely. Engineering difficulties were discovered and the beltway was moved farther up the river to its present location just beyond Cabin John.

A new highway, Clara Barton Parkway, was built in the 1960s from near Great Falls to Washington, parallel to the canal. Another highway, Cabin John Parkway, was built under the Union Arch Bridge as a connector from the beltway to Clara Barton Parkway.

Ralph Springmann, an early resident of Cabin John, remembered how the area looked before the Clara Barton Parkway. "It was country, and it was restful....But when you start making a bunch of improvements and putting roads through and things like that, it takes away the old charm. Before the parkway was built, I used to like to walk back – my lot reached the canal then – and sit on the bank of the canal...There wasn't a noise; there weren't cars like now; and no airplanes. And the streetcars – why, they were perfectly satisfactory. There was a funny thing about the streetcars: You could tell when one had reached the end of the line. For some reason, your lights would dim."

Courtesy Gerald Quinn

Cabin John Parkway was built under the Union Arch Bridge as a connector from the beltway to Clara Barton Parkway.

No description of the area of Cabin John is complete without telling what it is not. Cabin John Creek starts beyond Cabin John in Rockville, Maryland, and flows through North Potomac. Perhaps that is why a shopping center in North Potomac was given the name Cabin John Mall. A middle school in North Potomac, Md., is also named Cabin John and a county park is named Cabin John Regional Park. None of these are part of Cabin John, Maryland.

An area without borders in earlier days, Cabin John, Maryland, today is a distinct community, with its own zip code, 20818, bordered by roads to the north, west and east, and to the south, by the river and canal.

Courtesy Andy Rice

Clara Barton Parkway provides access to Cabin John.

Chapter 3
Rural to Residential

When Captain John Smith sailed up the Potomac River he found an area sparsely populated and used for hunting and fishing by Native Americans. Before his arrival, the "area had been inhabited for centuries," Andrew Rice wrote in Cabin John's *The Village News*, "indeed, for millennia."

Archeologists date the earliest habitation to about 8000 BC or the Archaic Period. A site on Ruppert Island, southeast of today's Cabin John near Glen Echo, has been identified as part of the Susquehannah Soapstone Culture dating to 1600 BC. Among the American Indians of the region were the Piscataways, who were members of the Algonquin tribe, the Susquehannocks and the Senecas. While there was no permanent Native American settlement where Cabin John exists now, artifacts from Indian culture have been found in Cabin John.

In 1634, another explorer, Henry Fleete, also came up the Potomac River to Little Falls, close to Cabin John. He wrote, "This place is without question the most pleasant in all this country and most convenient for habitation; the air temperate in summer and not violent in winter...the soil is exceedingly fertile; but above this place the country is rocky and mountainous..."

The river and the surrounding forests provided sustenance to the earliest inhabitants. Later, the fertile land provided for European settlers. In 1742, the Maryland legislature paid 300 pounds to Indians to relinquish their land claim.

Settlement began slowly in the late 17th century and expanded in the 18th century. Land records show the area as part of Charles County at first, then part of Prince George's County in 1695, and part of Frederick County in 1748. The area became part of Montgomery County when it became a separate entity in 1776.

Early Land Owners

Until the 19th century, only a few families had settled in Cabin John, owning large tracts of land. In 1715, Captain Thomas Fletchall owned more than 100 acres known as Fletchall's Garden bordered for more than a thousand feet by Captain Johns Run, later called Captain Johns or Cabin John Creek. Edward Griffith in 1718 had surveyed and laid out 1,290 acres, "beginning at a bounded red oak standing on the west side of Captain Johns Run near the mouth of said run." But he died before completing payment for this grant and when his granddaughter, Mary Thompson, and her husband John tried to lay claim to the land 25 years later, in 1743, the grant had been divided.

In 1735, John Read patented 100 acres under the name of Reads Delight. In 1784, Joseph White bought Reads Delight and 35 acres of unclaimed land, calling it Bite the Biter. In 1793, Thomas Beall patented a land record for Halifax, between Fletchall's Garden and Bite the Biter, also bordered by Captain John's Creek. In 1802, Robert Peter patented Griffith Park with land that reached part of Carderock just west of Cabin John, angled back beyond Reads Delight.

The White family that had started with Bite the Biter continued to purchase land for farming. By 1840, all of the land that later became the main area of Cabin John and the Cabin John Park development was in the hands of Joseph G. White, grandson of Joseph White.

From Farms and Forests

After the Civil War, the White family began to sell off their farmland in pieces to Thomas Dowling, Joseph Bobinger and Thomas Tuohey. These three families determined the future of Cabin John.

J. S. Tomlinson brochure; courtesy Richard Cook

The American Land Company, owned by J. S. Tomlinson, bought most of Cabin John's open farmland to develop residential Cabin John Park in 1912.

23

Thomas Dowling's brother, William, purchased land in 1866 for a farm he named Graceland after his daughter. William Dowling built the tall white house with columns still standing on what is now 80th Street in Cabin John. Ten years later, Thomas bought more land nearby and deeded it to his wife Amanda. In the 1880s, she acquired the William Dowling home and other land parcels until she owned over 600 acres. In 1912, J. S. Tomlinson, president of the American Land Company, purchased all of the Dowling land for $50,000 for development of Cabin John Park.

In 1870, Joseph Bobinger bought 100 acres of the White property on the south side of the Conduit Road west of Cabin John Bridge. In 1876, the same year that Thomas and Amanda Dowling were expanding their farm, Thomas Tuohey bought 26 acres next to the Bobinger tract. In 1907, Charles Benson, an administrative judge and county commissioner of many talents, bought part of Thomas Tuohey's property. None of the

J.S. Tomlinson brochure; courtesy Richard Cook

Above: Thomas Tuohey's house in 1913.

Right: The Tuohey house in 2007.

Tim Shank

24

Bobinger, Tuohey or Benson properties became part of the Cabin John Park development.

The Tuohey home was a tall white house on Conduit Road. Its location was marked on an 1878 map by G. M. Hopkins. In 1885, Dennis Tuohey, Thomas's son, purchased part of the Carderock tract. The Tuohey clan, considered by many to be Cabin John's "first family," ran a store that became a tavern and, after prohibition, a "beer joint." Tuoheys also founded and became leaders of the first fire department.

Near the turn of the 20th century, J. D. W. Moore sold five-acre plots at low cost to ten black families working on his farm. The road past these plots was called Number 10 until the county changed the name to Seven Locks Road. Henry Brown bought his farm for $300. His daughter, Miss Lena Brown, talked about the farm when she was 93. She recalled looking after chickens, turkeys and ducks while her father took vegetables from the farm to market in Washington. She later worked in the laundry at the Cabin John Bridge Hotel. The government bought her 4-1/2 acre property in 1940 to build housing for black workers at the nearby David Taylor Model Basin and it became known as Carver Road.

During the mid to late 1800s, Irish laborers hired to build the canal and then the bridge took squatters' rights near the river in shack-like cabins, abandoned canal boats and even trolley cars. They took water from hillside springs, grew small vegetable gardens, and hunted and fished. They frequented the tavern that started in part of the Tuohey home and shopped at Judge Benson's store. After the canal and bridge were finished, they worked on area farms. Later, some were early volunteers for the first fire department.

By 1910, Cabin John seemed to have only six houses according to Thomas Tuohey's great-grandson Norman Tuohey.

"I'll start at the bridge, with the old Cabin John Bridge Hotel. The next thing you hit was Benson's store. On up the road, close to the road, an old house sits down on the bank to your left, just on the curve of where you get to the fire house. That...belonged to my great-grandfather. It has two rooms downstairs, stone basement, then frame construction – and two rooms up. That's three places. The next place was the house I was born in ...all that property from 79th Street clean over to Persimmon Tree Road was Dowling's farm, a big dairy farm; and the old house is still standing."

Josephine Havens remembered her childhood visits to Cabin John in 1912 when she would ride a horse across the creek and camp in a summer shack with her parents. "We had no lights, no electricity, and no running water. We carried our water up from the spring or from a well a block down the street..."

"Those hills were just covered with huge chestnut trees. Walnut and hickory and others too, but the chestnuts especially we came for. And persimmons. There were lots of persimmon trees all through this area. We used to bring our picnic lunch and stay all day. We'd take the chestnuts home and roast them."

Mrs. Havens also remembered the river and the canal. "...out here in the summer I swam, and we had our boat, a canoe, that we kept down at the lock. We went out on the river a lot: the river was clean and we could swim in it then.

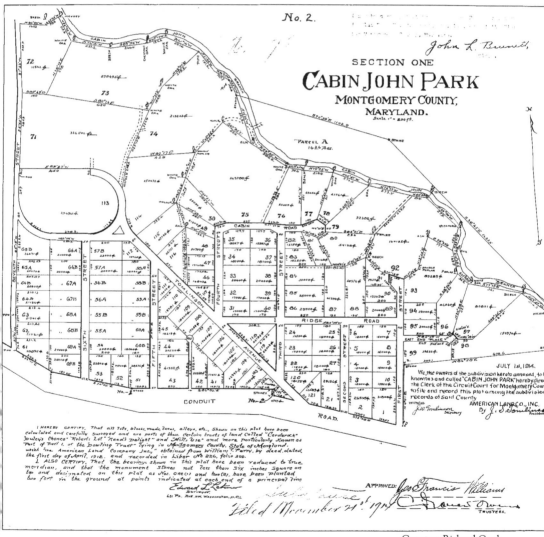

Map of Tract 1

"At that time everybody had gardens, vegetable gardens, and you worked in your family's garden and helped. We carried water, I'll tell you that! Of course the whole section where we lived had been farm anyway, but it hadn't been farmed for quite a while and the fields were all open."

Later, when she was in high school, her family moved to Cabin John. Back then, "there were a few more houses being built, but not many. We were pretty well isolated out here, so we had to depend on one another for company. There was no place to meet except at one another's houses; so we were what you might call very well chaperoned."

Cabin John Park

In 1912, the American Land Company began a development called Cabin John Park that would bring 600 new homes and replace the farms. J. S. Tomlinson,

3 Dozen Attractive Features
Cabin John Park

1. Near-City Homes	19. Grapes and Melons
2. Profitable Investments	20. Ginseng, Golden Seal
3. Splendid Location	21. All Garden Crops
4. Beautiful Home Sites	22. Chicken Farms
5. Villa, Bungalow Sites	23. High Elevation
6. Pleasant Surroundings	24. Monument in Sight
7. Attractive Scenery	25. Refreshing Breezes
8. Magnificent Situations	26. Sunshine and Shade
9. Surface Undulating	27. Abundant Shade Trees
10. Perfect Drainage	28. Healthy Community
11. Southern Exposure	29. Good Neighborhood
12. Fertile Land	30. Pure Spring Water
13. Suitable Truck Patches	31. Running Streams
14. Fruits and Vegetables	32. Best Public Roads
15. Fine Soil for Apples	33. Splendid Car Service
16. Peaches, Pears, Plums	34. Elec. Light, Telephone
17. Sweet, Irish Potatoes	35. Free Life Insurance
18. Lettuce, Kale and Cabbage	36. Cheap Prices and Liberal Terms

WRITE FOR FURTHER PARTICULARS

Courtesy Gerald Quinn

The American Land Company advertised the virtues of Cabin John Park in 1913.

owner of the company, bought the Dowling's 600 acres and laid out four sections of Cabin John Park. He began selling lots for $10 down and $10 a month. He advertised lots with at least 100 foot frontages, smaller lots with 15,000 to 40,000 square feet and larger lots one to five acres.

The sales brochure compared the area to new neighborhoods in Washington, D.C., and proclaimed that the "natural scenery is more romantic and fascinating than that in Rock Creek park and where there are more beautiful sites for country homes, villas, and bungalows than can be found at Cleveland Park or Chevy Chase." The development listed "3 Dozen Attractive Features," including "sunshine and shade," "refreshing breezes," "best public roads,"

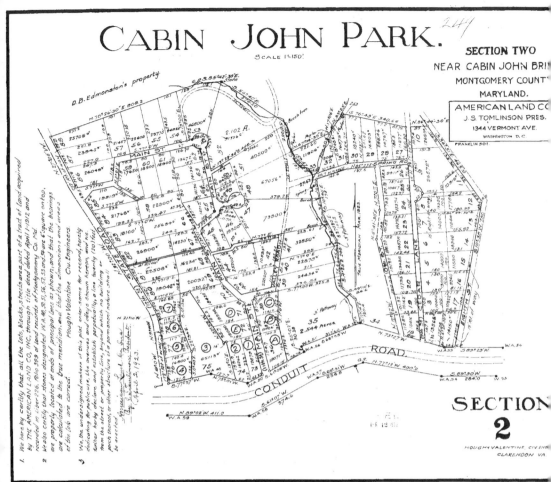

Map of Tract 2

"fertile land," and "splendid location" among others. A photo in the brochure is captioned, "Soil is splendid for Irish potatoes."

In 1913, the lots cost between 1 to 3 cents per square foot and ranged from $150 to $900 depending on size. A half-acre cost about $200. Tomlinson's brochure pointed out the investment potential of the area, noting that property in Cleveland Park in northwest Washington, D.C., and Chevy Chase, Maryland, was selling at 40 cents to 75 cents per square foot.

Cabin John Park was divided into four tracts or sections. Tract No. 1 contained 156 acres in a triangle shape beginning at the "big stone bridge over Cabin John Run" and bordered on the south by Conduit Road. It went from today's Cabin John Creek to Seven Locks Road. About three-fourths of the tract was one large open field and the remainder thickly forested with oak, hickory, dogwood, poplar and "a great many large and handsome Beech trees." It is interesting, as local history buff Richard Cook has noted, that no mention is made of chestnut trees, perhaps because a blight in Maryland three years earlier had wiped out most of the trees.

Tract No. 2 was west of Tract 1, from today's 79th Street to Persimmon Tree Road, with a "gradual slope for a fine view of the Potomac River and the Virginia Hills." Again to the west and adjoining it, Tract No. 3 also had a large field and farm crops. The early Friendship School was on the property. Tract No. 3, the most remote section, did not become developed.

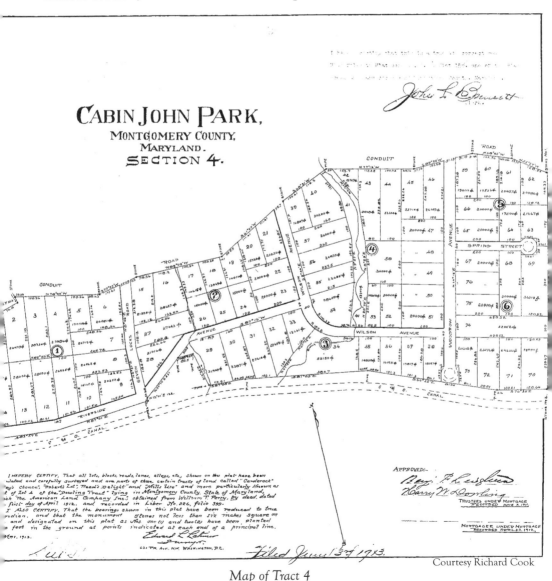

Courtesy Richard Cook

Map of Tract 4

Tract No. 4 was described as a "strip of land about 1,000 feet wide extending along the southside of the Conduit Road...and it borders along the Chesapeake and Ohio Canal." The land was described as "specially suited for small homes with chicken farms." Every lot had plenty of trees for shade and a park in the rear and "nearly every lot can be provided with fresh running spring water." In 1922, Section 4 was subdivided into Seven Locks Settlement which today encompasses 82nd Place, 83rd Place and 83rd Street.

Excavations had occurred in and around Cabin John in searches for gold. The American Land Company had to clear the title on some of the property because of an old deed covering the mineral rights. Perhaps for this reason or perhaps as a reminder of the pirate legends, Tomlinson cautioned that "In view of the probability of a future discovery of valuable deposits this company in selling the lots reserves one-half interest in all mineral rights." Some of the deeds contained this provision.

The first to purchase a lot in Section 4 was David S. Tuohey, grandson of Thomas Tuohey, and his wife Mary O'Brien Tuohey, who built their home on Woodrow Avenue (now 79th Street) in 1913. The lot and the house cost $2200.

That house now belongs to Barbara and Reed Martin. Jesse Crook, grandson of David and Mary Tuohey, grew up in the part of

David Tuohey built one of the first houses in Cabin John Park in 1913. The house today remains much as it was, carefully restored by owners Barbara and Reed Martin.

Tim Shank

Cabin John called Cabin John Gardens in the 1940s. He spent much time with his grandparents. Barbara Martin talked with Jesse, who has since moved away, and wrote, "David and Mary separated, and David lived in quarters above Tuohey's Tavern, the general store/ beer joint that he had taken over from his father. Mary operated the house on 79th Street as a boarding house. Jesse Crook recalls that his grandmother slept on a daybed in the living room, closed off by a curtain. Upstairs, six men had rooms Mrs. Tuohey served them breakfast and dinner, packed hearty lunches to carry to their jobs, and did their laundry. Not surprisingly, she never had a vacancy."

Charles Smith bought four lots and built his own house single-handed in 1913 on what is now 75th Street. He later helped Tomlinson build four other houses. He recalled the general state of Cabin John in those days: "...there was a school on Wilson Lane, about a quarter of a mile up from Conduit Road. And a school up on Persimmon Tree Road. There was a blacksmith's shop right at the corner of MacArthur Boulevard and Seven Locks. There was a Post Office at Tuohey's store. Tuohey's was just a country store, general merchandise, small groceries. And it was a place where people could let off their political opinions. ...And Gene [Charles] Benson had a blacksmith's shop. There was a lot of traffic on the Conduit Road then – horses, carriages, wagons...and usually one of the horses' shoes required attention."

Other early residents, Percy and Isabelle Redden, built three houses in Cabin John for her parents, brother and themselves. "It was my husband who got electric lights in Cabin John," said Mrs. Redden. "He went down to the electric company and they told him if he got, I think it was 15 signers as promised customers, they'd put electricity in for us. You know, it wasn't easy for him to get 15 signers. But he did. Three of them didn't have the money, and Mother and my husband paid their way and later we were paid back."

The Reddens also raised 250 white leghorn chickens, hatching them in a Sears Roebuck brooder that operated on kerosene. They also had four pigs. At that time, most people had chickens and many had a garden. For immediate needs, the Reddens shopped at Tuohey's store and took the trolley to Georgetown for staples.

At that time, streets all had different names. Halifax Street, likely named after the early land grant, is now 78th Street. Woodrow Avenue, which today is 79th Street, once continued to the canal. The current Woodrow Place was once named Spring Street. The numbered streets now begin mysteriously at 75th and end at 83rd, part of a numbering system that began in Washington, D.C., but never completed.

In 1913, gas was five cents a gallon and kerosene was three cents. Norman Tuohey's grandfather, Dennis Tuohey, had a 50-gallon drum of gasoline behind his store with a gallon measuring cup for people to measure, pay and dump the gasoline in their vehicle's tank. Bread also was a nickel. And, as Tuohey said, "You didn't sell milk. All the people living in the country in those days had an old cow, clean up to Depression time."

Early sales of Cabin John Park went slowly. Distance from Washington and development in the northwest section of the city to many seemed more attractive than traveling to Cabin John. The trolley also stopped at the bridge, limiting transportation to the Cabin John area. In 1915, the American Land Company continued its effort to develop Cabin John, selling 100 lots at auction for "little farms" on the north side of Conduit Road.

Cabin John Park also included some restrictions which were characteristic of the times. As the brochure explained, "To make and maintain a desirable standard for a new community means careful discrimination in many ways... One of these rules is that a deed or contract will not be made to a colored person and they will not be made to any other party until a majority of the five directors of the company are favorable to the proposed purchaser..." No meeting minutes or records suggest that restriction was ever observed.

Cabin John Park and Cabin John became synonymous names for the community, although in later years those with homes that were not

THE HAMPTON

SIX ROOMS AND BATH

*B*ungalow architecture features the Hampton. The interior is designed along practical lines. Full use of space affords a greater amount of room than is usual in a house of this size. The location of each room and its relation to the rest of the house have been planned to promote the comfort of the family.

Details and features: Six rooms and one bath. Full-width front porch with hipped roof and tapered wood columns; exposed roof rafter tails; glazed front door.

Years and catalog numbers: 1925 (3208); 1926 (P3208); *1928 (C3208)*; 1929 (P3208)

Price: $1,551 to $1,681

Similar to: The Grant

Difference: Slightly simpler detailing

Years and catalog numbers: 1925 (6018); *1926 (P6018)*; 1928 (C6028)

Price: $947 to $999

The Sullivan family built a "Hampton" model Sears kit house in 1925 that remains in pristine condition today.

Courtesy Marion Sullivan

part of the development fiercely defended being part of Cabin John, not Cabin John Park. It was not until the 1960s that the citizens association and the newsletter casually stopped using Cabin John Park and the community became known simply as Cabin John. Only the fire department, no longer located in Cabin John, continues to be named Cabin John Park Volunteer Fire Department.

In 1925, the Cabin John Park Citizens Association took a mid-summer census and reported a total population of 466, of whom 80 were identified as "summer residents." There were 130 families and 198 resident property owners.

In 1930, a census for Cabin John Park showed 595 people, including 63 African Americans. There were 149 households, including 19 African American families, all but four living on Seven Locks Road. Many households contained extended family members and several had lodgers. Occupations reflected the middle class makeup of the community. Some 37 people worked for the government in a variety of positions, such as engineers, economists, scientists, clerks, laborers, and a custodian at the Lincoln Memorial. There was only one farmer and one blacksmith, but 19 carpenters.

Houses

Prices for lots in Cabin John started rising in the 1920s, even as the Depression years began. Ralph Springmann, another early resident, paid a thousand dollars for an acre in 1929. He reminisced in the mid-1970s about those early years in Cabin John. "The lot I bought in 1929 was just covered with growth – blackberry bushes and everything you could think of....and we worked and cleared quite a bit of the lot, enough for the house to be built. When I built my house, the neighborhood was all but empty...

"I got the design for the house from a young fellow David Tuohey knew. It's a well-built house; it's a strong house; cinderblock and practically fireproof. We had a forty-foot well blasted and it never went dry.

"I used to visit out here from 1921 until we built in 1929. Of course there was no television then, and the only thing people had were radios, crystal sets. Finally they had sets that would run by batteries...There were church socials and things like that. They would have cake sales at the church, and chicken dinners...They'd serve these dinners at tables at the Methodist Church. And when the firehouse was built, they gave dances every Saturday night.

"And people used to visit one another. Everybody had a good time and we just mixed and mingled...there just isn't the friendly feeling that we used to have."

Charles and Jennie Sullivan bought four lots in Section Two for themselves and their three sons. They built two Sears kit houses next door to each other, the "Hampton" and the "Grand" models, on Persimmon Tree Road. Grandson Thomas "Billy" Sullivan was born in one of the houses, and years later, he moved back to his "Granny" Sullivan's house with his wife Marion.

"When they built the second aqueduct, people came from all over the United States to work on that project and Granny Sullivan would feed them here, sometimes 5 or 6, and they would sleep here in the summer on the back porch. She would cook for them. Later, some of them came back to visit her. This was in the 1920s," said Marion Sullivan, recalling how Granny talked about those days.

Marion added, "Granny Sullivan saw the horse and buggy into the jet age." Jennie Sullivan and her husband owned a "pop stand" at Great Falls where they would sell hot dogs and soda. "She used to say when she was a child she could walk across the falls to the Virginia side. She also told the story that during the Civil War, her brother was sitting outside a red stone building at Great Falls when a bullet came whizzing over his head into the door. The bullet hole is still there," Marion recounted. Later, the pop stand was moved to 81st Street in Cabin John as a home for one of Granny's sons.

Left: The Sullivan family built two Sears kit houses in Cabin John Park, including this one in 1920.

Below: The Hornauers renovated the Sullivan's 1920 Sears house, keeping the front rooms and porch just as they were.

Courtesy Elaine Hornauer

Tim Shank

Both photos courtesy Marion Sullivan

Above: Granny Sullivan's pop stand was moved from Great Falls Tavern to Cabin John where it became part of a house.

Right: Granny Jenny Sullivan (far left) and family members.

In 1986, resident and retired Smithsonian Institution modeler Reed Martin led a walking tour of 25 Sears kit houses in Cabin John. Sears sold these homes by catalog from 1910 to 1937. They were shipped pre-fabricated and assembled locally. At least 20 different models were represented in Cabin John, most built during the 1920s. In recent years, a number of these original homes have been taken down and entirely new homes built in their place in the style of vintage homes.

During the 1930s, Chris Gates built a fine brick and frame house for his wife and two daughters next to Lock 8 and the lockhouse. His brother John and his son, Boots Gates, crippled by polio and one of the "characters" well known at Tuohey's bar, lived in a lesser home nearby.

Christine Gates Cerniglia and her sister Kathleen Gates Carroll remember swimming in the canal. Even though they were young girls, they also remember that their home was taken by the state in the late 1950s to construct part of the Dulles Interceptor sewer line.

35

Above: Tim Shank;
Right: courtesy Uva Worsham Cable

Above: The Reddings, who brought electricity to Cabin John, also built a Sears kit house in the 1920s, later owned by the Worshams and then by their daughter Uva Worsham Cable.

Right: Young Lynda Worsham, Pat Tuohey, baby Doug Cable, and Joan Shuff were photographed in the 1930s with Conduit Road and the Marshall family house behind them. The house is where MacArthur Plaza stands today.

Below left: Like other Cabin John children, the Gates sisters – (left to right) Kathleen and Christine – would swim and play in the canal.

Bottom: In the 1940s, Chris Gates built a house on the C&O Canal next to Lockhouse 8.

Photos courtesy Christine Gates Cerniglia

Courtesy Christine Gates Cerniglia

Chris Gates holds his daughter Christine as a canal pleasure boat goes through Lock 8 in the 1940s.

The action was necessary to prevent raw sewage from entering the river at Cabin John. Still, the Gates family never got over losing their home by the canal. Today, while the river may be cleaner, and efforts are underway to address the problem, the sewer line expels a stench at various times to that area of the towpath that the D. C. Water and Sewer Authority has never managed to dispel.

The eclectic nature of Cabin John and the independence of its residents were evident in the houses they built. In 1923, Harry and Olive Humphrey built an entirely different house on two acres of land at the end of what is now 76th Street. Dr. Humphrey, a plant pathologist for the U.S. Department of Agriculture, had read about rammed earth construction in South Africa. He liked the idea of saving money by building a house by compacting or "ramming" a mixture of clay, sand, gravel and soil that he could dig right from his own property.

With labor from family members, he dug the basement and set the concrete block foundation and then rammed the clay, gravel and soil mixture into wooden forms to

Tim Shank

Rammed earth house.

37

form the walls of the first floor with space for windows and doors. Rammed earth construction is known in some Western states but while a misnomer, the house in Cabin John may be the oldest "mud house" in the County.

The house has the further distinction of having hosted Hubert Humphrey, a nephew, on his first visit to Washington. It was after sitting in the Senate gallery that Hubert wrote to his fiancée, Muriel Buck, "I can see how some day, if you and I just apply ourselves and make up our minds to work for bigger things, we can live here in Washington and probably be in government, politics or service. I set my aim at Congress." Hubert Humphrey was elected to the Senate 13 years later in 1948 and in 1965 became Vice President of the United States.

In 1951, the rammed earth house was purchased by Dr. George L. Weil, the nuclear scientist who, working with Dr. Enrico Fermi in Chicago in 1942, removed a cadmium-plated rod from uranium and graphite causing the first nuclear chain reaction. In Cabin John, he erected a tall radio tower on the property to transmit calls from scientists stationed in Antarctica.

An architect, Rocky Wood, built himself a house made of hewn logs in the 1930s, overlooking the C&O Canal and Potomac River in Cabin John. The logs, rescued from an old Pennsylvania farmhouse, are painted white and a matching smaller building, like a gatehouse, sits on Riverside Drive. Part of the gatehouse was a forge, and its use is reflected in the hinges, handles and latches of the house.

Courtesy Maryland National Capital Park and Planning Commission (MNCPPC)
Log house.

Villa house.

Betty and Charley Thompson moved into the house in the 1950s and continued to preserve it and beautify the property. Dr. Thompson became president of the Cabin John Park Fire Board. Today, their son Toby, now a writer and Pennsylvania State University professor, lives in the house.

Cabin John has attracted other architects including Jim Wilner, Tom Manion, Bob Wilkoff, David Brown and Bill Neudorfer who have designed and built their own homes and those of many neighbors. The Wilner home resembles a Tuscan villa. The Manions remodeled their house into a classic arts and crafts home.

Another architect, Charles Goodman, who also designed the original National Airport terminal, designed a house that was altered over the years. The present owner, Gerald Quinn, restored the house on Arden Road back to the original mid-century modern design.

Modern house.

Tommy and Naomi Denell bought a two-bedroom "package house" in 1956 from the Washington, D.C., hardware company Barber and Ross. They added a second bathroom and third bedroom. Tommy's grandfather had been the lockkeeper at Lock 7 and his father had been born in that lockhouse.

Tommy and Naomi Denell, 2007.

Judy Welles

Naomi recalled, "People said, 'why do you want to live in Cabin John?' I said, number one it's something we can afford; number two, our kids can walk to school; number three, we live close to Bethesda if I choose to go there to work, and number four, there was no traffic. Over the years all of that has changed."

Tommy added, "Everybody at that point in time wanted to move to Wheaton or Kensington. They was bustin' open." These communities seemed more accessible and desirable locations in the 1950s.

In the 1960s and 70s, other unusual houses appeared, including a domed house. More recently, a few modernist and angular houses have appeared. Among unique structures in one backyard is a tiny one-room chapel with a large stained-glass window. Built in the 1930s,

Tim Shank

Dome house.

at one time it was the smallest consecrated chapel in the United States according to a Ripley's Believe It or Not cartoon.

On a nearby street is a post-and-beam garage – one of few of that old-time construction in the county – that was hand-milled by the owner, Evan Mater, from two huge poplar trees and an oak that fell

into the yard during a storm. Evan lives in the house his parents bought in 1948 from the family that owned a quarry in Cabin John.

For some, construction has focused on restoring and remodeling Cabin John's vintage houses. For developers, tearing down old houses for the valuable land and

Tim Shank

New house, 2007.

building much larger Victorian-style homes have taken many of the Sears houses and changed the pastoral look of Cabin John.

Cabin John Gardens

Events in the 1930s and 40s put Cabin John on the map again and increased the population. In 1936, the Navy began constructing the David Taylor Model Basin at Carderock, completing it in 1939. It later became part of the Carderock Division of the Naval Surface Warfare Center.

The original site planned for the Model Basin had been in Cabin John. In fact, in December 1940, the federal government purchased 19.27 acres of land west of Cabin John Creek and south of Conduit Road from Mary Ellen Bobinger, widow of William H. Bobinger, owner of the Cabin John Bridge Hotel. But instead of building a model basin on this site, the government, responding to housing shortages and gas rationing, used the property to build housing for workmen at the Model Basin. These homes were the only residential construction in Montgomery County during World War II, and Cabin John's population grew.

The Navy had 125 homes constructed in Cabin John – 100 for white workers and 25 for black. The two small neighborhoods – Cabin John Gardens off MacArthur Boulevard and Carver Road off Seven Locks Road – became important parts of the larger Cabin John community as the years passed.

Courtesy MNCPPC

Cabin John Gardens was built in the early 1940s, where the Cabin John Bridge Hotel once stood, to house workers from the David Taylor Model Basin.

Unlike other Cabin John streets which are mostly numbered, streets in Cabin John Gardens are named for naval engineers and architects, including Ericsson, Froude, Thorne, McKay, Russell, and Webb.

Sir William Froude pioneered model testing in the United Kingdom, which became the basis for Admiral David Taylor's later work in ship construction. John Ericsson was a Swedish naval engineer who designed the U.S.S. *Monitor*, a Union Navy ironclad warship used in the Civil War. John Russell designed the first seagoing battleship made entirely of iron in the mid 1800s. William Webb designed commercial ships in the 1800s. Donald McKay designed some of the grandest and most successful clipper ships ever built, including the Flying Cloud and the Sovereign of the Seas in the mid-1800s.

At first, the government rented Cabin John Gardens housing to Model Basin employees. Machine shop technician Jack Widmayer and his brother Lincoln worked in the Model Basin's wood shop and lived "in one of those government houses with a cement floor." Some 75 of the homes had two bedrooms and 25 had three bedrooms. They all had coal furnaces and the first private sewer system in the county. There was also a Community House for social events and Scout meetings.

Marion Scott Sullivan, one of three children of Clarence and Clarabell Scott, also remembers growing up in the Gardens. Her father was a machinist at the Model Basin.

"Everybody knew everybody and everybody knew all about everybody. As my father used to say to me, 'young lady, I don't care where you are at or what you are doing, you may not know who is looking at you, but they know who you are.' You never did anything wrong because if you did someone would say they saw you."

In those days, she could almost name every person on both sides of the Garden. "Now I hardly know anyone," she said.

With World War II and returning veterans in the mid-1940s, the Gardens expanded its policies to rent to veterans.

Even in the 1950s, the area was still rural. Wayne Swisher, a Cabin John Gardens resident who worked as a photographer for the Army Map Service and then as a stonemason, said, "We were out in the country where there was still horses and chickens." His daughter Dana Swisher Lupton, who returned to live in "the Gardens" as an adult, remembers how everyone in the neighborhood was "like family" and "there was a lot of things for kids to do." Another resident, David Fyock, remembers the short walk to the river where he fished for perch, bass, catfish and scrappy. His mother, LaVeta Fyock, did hairdressing in her home for the neighbors.

In 1955, the Navy Department gave notice to residents that the Public Housing Administration had decided to sell the project to 1) residents individually, 2) to residents cooperatively, or 3) to the highest bidder. On December 2, 1955, the Cabin John Gardens Citizens Association was formed and residents began writing letters to urge the County Council to allow individual purchase of the houses. The campaign was heated, and at one point it was reported that the Cabin John Citizens Association was opposed to the Gardens, asking for removal of the tenants and disposition of the property.

Finally, in 1956, when the County Council would not approve sale of the property as individual housing, the property was offered for sale on a cooperative basis. A corporation, Cabin John Gardens, Inc., was formed to set a price for each house and draw up by-laws and membership agreements.

Reminiscing 20 years later, Dagny Newman, Secretary of the Cabin John Gardens Board of Directors, wrote, "We formed various committees and had our lawyer work out drafts for members and by-laws that we could go over and then have an overall meeting to discuss matters with the residents who desired to buy. When I think back and go over some of the old papers I wonder how we had the nerve to even try to do all these things – but do them we did and very satisfactorily too."

The government sold the 100 homes for $490,000, with owners becoming members of Cabin John Gardens, Inc. The plan was for each member homebuyer to pay a down payment of $847 or $968, depending on whether the house had two or three bedrooms, and a monthly installment of $53 or $60.

In 1957, 76 residents became proud owners of homes in the hard fought-for Cabin John Gardens, Inc. The Gardens today is the only cooperative single-family housing in Montgomery County. Members own their houses but not the land on which the houses stand. The Corporation takes care of taxes, street and sewer maintenance, and any community problems that concern members. Over the years, coal furnaces changed to some oil, some gas, and some electricity for heating, all contracted by the cooperative.

There have been few changes in the original documents of the cooperative. Thelma Marshall, who became manager for the cooperative in the 1960s, was one of the first owners with her husband Pearman. Still living in Cabin John Gardens, she said, "We have a manager and board of directors that meets twice a month. We have to fix a water main break ourselves; we have to clean the streets when it snows."

Improvements in homes and remodeling required more letter writing campaigns to county officials, and it began to take less time for building permits. Houses became larger with upper stories and additions on the side and back. Once very small and uniform, Gardens houses today have many different sizes, shapes and styles.

Children and grandchildren of many of the original owners have come back and purchased homes in the community with a hallmark for being close-knit. Children who grew up in the Gardens "never had to worry about mother not being home when they came home from school as there was always the house next door or up the road where they could go and be welcome," wrote Newman.

Mrs. Marshall lived in the Gardens with her husband and four children in a two-bedroom house. She recalled, "When our kids were young, there was no parkway, just woods, and we had a path that went down to the canal. It was much nicer then without the parkway. We had raccoons – I haven't seen one in a long time. Back in those days we used to have more time with the kids than it seems like people have today. We had Halloween parties, party with Santa Claus, cook-outs."

She also remembered the closeness of the community. "We more or less looked after one another. If there was illness, we would look after whoever. Even collecting money to help."

Carver Road

Like Cabin John Gardens, Carver Road also had a close-knit community, a cluster of 20 African-American families. Of the families who moved there, many are still there, as adult children and grandchildren stayed on. Many of Cabin John's strongest leaders have come from Carver Road residents and the Cabin John community has a legacy of close and supportive relationships.

Courtesy MNCPPC

In the early 1940s, the federal government built 20 houses on Carver Road for black workers at the Model Basin.

Frank McKinney moved his family to a house on Carver Road in 1943, paying $28 a month rent, and he later bought the house. He worked for the Army Map Service and became active at Gibson Grove AME Zion Church and in the Cabin John community, where he served as vice president of the citizens association.

He recalled how weekends in Cabin John were times for families to be together. "After church, everybody would spend Sunday pitching horseshoes, eating a big dinner. The kids would swim in Cabin John Creek. Sometimes the youngsters would go down to the Potomac to swim; that was in the 30s and early 40s when the water was cleaner."

"I was part of Cabin John before I was born," Bill White told Barbara Martin for an article in February, 1985, *The Village News*. "My grandparents and my parents lived here and I was born here. There are black families that have lived around Cabin John for a hundred years and more."

Bill became co-chairman of the Home Study program with Celeste Swedenburg in the 1960s. The Home Study group tutored and provided homework assistance to Carver Road children when the transition to integrated schools occurred and for many years afterwards. Celeste told *The Village News*, "Black kids were being kicked out of school on a daily basis. They needed individual help and encouragement. I planned it with a lady I was working for. She found tutors and I found the students."

Tutors would come to the children's homes and study with them regularly. The group also got school clothes for the children if they were needed. Home Study graduates were even helped with college expenses through a grant program. The Home Study program continued for about 25 years.

In 1970, they decided to have a crab feast as a fundraiser for the program. The first Crab Feast, and many subsequent gatherings, were held in the field behind White's backyard. For eight years, the Crab Feast was put on entirely by the Carver Road community. As the attendance increased into the hundreds, the Citizens Association joined in to help, and, in 1990, the event was moved to the Clara Barton Community Center. Many Cabin John residents remember the taste of the collards, baked beans, green beans and potato salad that could never be really replicated even though the women of Carver Road shared the recipes.

Some of the organizers of the first Crab Feast in 1970 were (left to right) Diane Leatherman, Frank McKinney, Margaret Cole, Bill White (seated), Celeste Swedenburg, Peter Vogt and Lena Rose.

Courtesy Gerald Quinn

Also during this time, Palisades Pool was built off Seven Locks Road near Carver Road. White, active in the Citizens Association, requested that the pool's management begin the Cabin John Free Swim program. As a result, Cabin John residents are allowed to use the pool free of charge twice a week, from 11 a.m. to 1 p.m.

Beginning in 1998, homeowners in Carver Road began replacing their small houses with larger, more modern homes. Some sold their homes and even larger homes were built by new residents on the lots.

Community Plan

When the Clara Barton Parkway was planned, thought was given to a cutoff from the beltway to the parkway that would have included a triangular piece of ground including nearly all of Cabin John. The Bogley Realty Company made the radical proposal that this triangle would be an attractive location to develop a high-rise shopping center complex with a motel, apartments and townhouses.

On July 26, 1959, the *Washington Post* reported that the Bogley scheme "could ultimately wipe out all of the existing riverside Montgomery County community and take over additional undeveloped acreage." Then, on August 4, the Post reported that "the Maryland National Park and Planning Commission staff views the project as the first major effort to crack the Cabin John watershed master plan."

The Bogley company, as recalled by Citizen Association President John Jessup, interviewed residents on their interest in selling their properties to the company. Many did not want to be uprooted or see anything wipe out Cabin John. But some saw the proposal as favorable to them economically, and opinion was divided in the community. Elizabeth Kytle wrote that "the situation became so tense that in some cases longstanding friendships were broken on the rock of the Bogley proposal."

One resident, Mrs. Don Iglehart, told a reporter that "These people keep talking about progress and feel sorry for us," she said. "They say we're five miles away from where we can buy a loaf of bread. Well, we like it that way. That's why we came."

The Cabin John Citizens Association called a special meeting at the request of the realty company. Interest was so high that the location was changed from the Cabin John Recreation Center to the firehouse auditorium.

It was a crowded noisy meeting at which "voices were raised, fingers shaken, and accusations flung about quite freely – a favorite accusation being, 'You're keeping me from making a fortune!'" But a show of hands vote clearly proved that at least 75 percent of the community disapproved of the company's proposal. The project was abandoned.

In the late 1960s and early 1970s, real estate developers became interested in several unused tracts of land in Cabin John for high density housing. In 1970, the population of Cabin John had increased to 1,604 among 481 households. Compared to the rest of Montgomery County, Cabin John had a higher percentage of people over 55, including 41 who were older than 75. The median house value was $25,000 compared to the county median of $33,000. Houses were also smaller, with five rooms compared to six on average in the county. Children up to high school age comprised one-third of the population.

Concerned about the potential effects of development on the ecology and life style of the area, the residents began a community planning effort in 1967 with the Montgomery County Department of Community Development. By 1970, a Cabin John Development Corporation was formed to implement specific community proposals, and in 1971, a community survey was conducted.

The Cabin John Citizens Association circulated a questionnaire to all households asking residents to express their views on the kind of Cabin John they wanted. The questionnaire produced a 55 percent return with a diversity of views. But it was still clear, according to Andy Rice, "that the majority wanted to preserve Cabin John's unique character of a mixed socio-economic population in a rather rural setting, although with some definite improvements in public services."

The next step was to set up Survey Action Committees to take the survey results and propose specific courses of action. Five committees were formed – on housing, land use, natural resources, public improvements and public services – which had sub-groups on education, health, day care, library and recreation. With the assistance of a community planner from the Department of Community Development, the committees spent months defining priorities.

Finally, in 1973, a community plan was drafted and presented at two town meetings. Residents reached agreement on a community plan that was subsequently incorporated into the Bethesda-Chevy Chase Master Plan. The Cabin John Community Plan culminated three years of community effort directed toward future self-determination. Signed by D. Edwin Winslow, "President of Cabin John Park Citizens Association 1972-1973," the document stated, "...this Cabin John Community Plan contains our goals, objectives and proposals for the future of the area in which we live – and the assertion that we, the citizens, have both the right and the duty to direct the lifestyle we choose to follow, rather than have it done for us." As it had in the past, the Cabin John community determined its own future and the Community Plan became a major factor in preserving the Cabin John "way of life."

The plan began with an introduction to the area. Excerpts describe the community's vision and values:

"Bounded by major highways and the Potomac River, the 450 acres in this triangle provide a unique setting and life style....Future development of vacant land tracts in Cabin John, hold promise of a 60 to 70 percent increase in total population, putting immense pressure on the socio-economic character of the area...

"Cabin John is a widely diverse community of social, economic and racially mixed citizens, houses, and institutions. A community survey indicated that residents prefer this diversity and became the basis for establishing plan goals. Thus the prime goal of the planning activity is to preserve the existing life style and heterogeneity from predatory encroachments by land speculators, developers, and high density users...

"The values Cabin John residents most often express a desire to maintain are: a quiet atmosphere, small town friendliness, many trees, the unique mix of economic levels, varied housing stock, and racial and cultural diversity. In an era when many other local communities are attempting to make themselves homogeneous, Cabin John is actively attempting to maintain its diversity."

An appendix to the Community Plan documented the natural landscape of Cabin John because of the strong role it played in the community. "Visitors often express surprise and admiration of the green surroundings and for the past 40 years District botanists have roamed the woods for specimens."

The paper noted that the dominant native trees are oak, hickory, tulip poplar and sycamores with less dominant varieties of elm, walnut, butternut, swamp maple, persimmon and box elder among others. Along with numerous ferns, the "woods and fields abound with wild flowers. In spring there are bloodroot, phlox, violets, hepatica, Dutchman's breeches, squirrel corn, trout lilies, Virginia bluebells, jack-in-the-pulpit, and wild ginger. In summer, there are daisies, black-eyed susan, clover, mellilot, butterfly weed and common milkweed; in the fall, there are asters, hawkweed, goldenrod, and gentians." Other plants were described as being in Cabin John so long that they are generally assumed to be native, including a variety of fruit trees, mulberry, boxwood, paulownia, dame's rocket, pine and spruce.

Judy Welles

Cabin John Creek

The plan included a zoned commercial area, previously lacking in the community, which resulted in the development of today's MacArthur Plaza shopping center. There were dozens of recommendations, from zoning of undeveloped tracts to coin-operated lights on the tennis courts.

Even after the Community Plan, the proper place for commercial development was a continuing issue for many years. In 1974, several properties in Cabin John were downzoned from commercial to residential zoning because the Community Plan had envisioned consolidating all commercial uses in one location, the Tuohey tract. But protests arose from people who had commercial operations that they did not want zoned residential. The issue became so heated that over 170 people turned out for a meeting in 1975 at which two county policemen were on hand. Downzoning was defeated at the meeting.

In 1975, on wooded land that lay undeveloped on the west side of Persimmon Tree in Cabin John, opposite Caraway Street, Berger Berman company began construction of 89 contemporary-style homes on what was called the Lemm Tract. The construction provided open wooded space and preserved trees on every lot. The neighborhood called itself Persimmon Tree rather than the official and pretentious name of the development, Country Club Estates. The community also opted to use the West Bethesda postal zip code 20817 instead of Cabin John's 20818.

During the 1970s, a small apartment building was built with a view to housing for senior members of the community. The building later was turned into condo units for residents of all ages.

More development followed in 1982 when Porten Sullivan began construction of 45 townhouses on 12.5 acres of the Polinger Tract that became known as MacArthur Park. The development brought

Tim Shank

MacArthur Park brought townhouses to Cabin John.

Tim Shank

MacArthur House condo apartment building next to Captain's Market.

150 new residents to Cabin John. Susan Roberts, who has lived in the neighborhood for 20 years, said, "With woods in the back, I have felt like I was on vacation ever since I moved here." A retired District of Columbia police detective, Susan now teaches piano and, with Andy Rice on cello and two friends who are flutists, she plays in a classical music group called "Divertimento."

Also in 1982, the Hufty Tract north of the water tower on Seven Locks Road was developed for 31 townhouses on Archbold Terrace known as Seven Locks Overlook.

The 2000 census found the community continuing to grow, although the population of children under 18 declined to 27 percent. There were 1734 people living in Cabin John, including 63 African Americans – curiously the same number as in 1930.

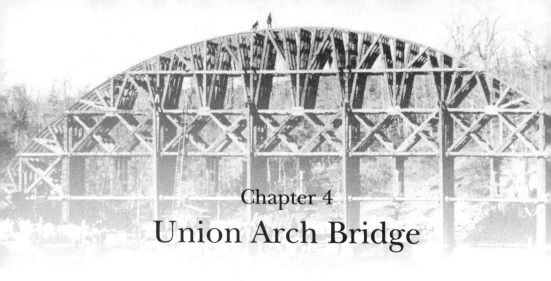

Chapter 4
Union Arch Bridge

The Union Arch Bridge, also called the Cabin John Bridge, is an engineering marvel. It was originally designed for the aqueduct carrying water from the Potomac River to Washington, D.C, a monumental achievement in itself. When it was built, the bridge was the longest single-span stone arch in the world, a record that continued for 40 years. Today it is the longest in the United States and third longest in the world.

The bridge is 450 feet long, 20 feet four inches wide, and 100 feet high, with an arch span of 220 feet. Built by the Army Corps of Engineers from 1857 to 1863 at a cost of $254,000, the bridge stands in tribute to its designer and developer, Capt. Montgomery C. Meigs, a man of many talents who later became a Brigadier General.

U.S. Army Corps of Engineers
Capt. Montgomery C. Meigs.

Among Meigs' accomplishments were completion of the Washington Aqueduct, redesign of the Capitol dome, location of Arlington National Cemetery, and design of the elegant Pension Building, now the National Building Museum in Washington, D.C.

In 1851, a Christmas Eve fire destroyed part of the Capitol building and there wasn't enough water to put out the fire in time. A year later, with memory of that devastating fire, Congress recognized that the nation's capital needed more than wells and springs for its water and appropriated $100,000 for a survey and first steps for an aqueduct.

In November, 1853, ground was broken at Great Falls for the first public water system for Washington.

The Plan

Meigs' plan was to divert the water from the Potomac River at Great Falls into a nine-foot diameter brick conduit that would be 12 miles long. Gravity and pumping stations would direct water through the conduit to retaining reservoirs where it could then be pumped to the city's pipelines. With the population of Washington at about 58,000, water needs were estimated at about 5,220,000 gallons per day. The conduit was designed for a capacity of 76,500,000 gallons of water daily.

Six bridges were built as part of the original Washington Aqueduct water system to carry the conduit over streams and creeks. Bridge No. 3, also named the Griffith Park Bridge which goes over Mountain Spring Branch, is a smaller version of the Union Arch bridge. It is 200 feet long with an arch spanning 75 feet. Both bridges are in full view in Cabin John. The Union Arch bridge rises over Cabin John Creek and Cabin John Parkway, and Bridge No. 3 is off MacArthur Boulevard just past Persimmon Tree Road.

Tim Shank

Above: Bridge No. 3, completed in 1858, is the smallest of two aqueduct bridges in Cabin John.

Right: Bridge No. 3 in 1913.

J. S. Tomlinson; courtesy Richard Cook

Some think Bridge No. 3 was built as a working model for the larger Union Arch bridge. But the arch is elliptical, unlike the Union Arch. The road does not go over the smaller bridge which seems to abut a large hill. This was once called Indian Hill because it was thought that Native Americans climbed to the top to gaze out over the early landscape. Today, Cabin John residents walk across Bridge No. 3 with pets or jog and bike across to a bike path on the other side of MacArthur Boulevard.

Judy Welles
A walking/biking path goes over Bridge No. 3.

Plans for the Union Arch Bridge were first prepared by Alfred L. Rives and approved by Capt. Meigs. Soon after work on the bridge began, Rives was placed in charge of the construction by Meigs and remained on the work until 1861 when he resigned to join the Confederate Army. Disturbed by Rives action, Meigs did not permit the engineer's name to be carved onto the bridge below his own name.

The most serious obstacle to the aqueduct occurred at Cabin John Creek. Engineers found a ravine that was too wide and deep to fill. At first Meigs considered spanning the valley with a series of piers and arches supporting a masonry bridge. But after studying several examples he chose the single arch, as reported in the Corps of Engineers history of the aqueduct. Hidden inside the side walls are five spandrel arches at the west end of the bridge and four at the east end to relieve the load. The brick conduit, enclosed in stone, rested on top of the arch.

The Project

The project began as workmen blasted away the hillside until the solid ledge of rock was exposed and made ready for the supports for the bridge. Meigs also realized he needed an economical way to transport the needed heavy timbers and stone. The C&O Canal crossed the Cabin John Valley about 1,000 feet south of where he had planned to span the valley. The first step was to dam Cabin John Creek and build a lock to connect it to the C&O Canal. Barges

brought the wood and heavy stone construction materials from
Seneca, along the canal, through the diverted lock to the site.

The bridge abutments are gneiss from a quarry Meigs opened just
upstream from the bridge, interior spandrel arches and the parapet
walls (added later in 1872) are sandstone from Seneca, and the arch
ring has cut granite stones from Quincy, Massachusetts. Bridge
workers also quarried some of the abutment stone a few hundred feet
up the valley at quarries still operating today.

At the project site, derricks hoisted the timbers and stone into
place. A trestle was erected in the shape of an arch frame to bear the
arch stones and another trestle was built to carry the stones to their
places, but the derricks proved effective.

Courtesy Richard Cook
A wooden trestle supported the arch during construction of the Union Arch Bridge.

During construction of the Union Arch Bridge, Meigs rode
his horse "Corbo" or traveled in a Washington Aqueduct carriage,
equipped with runners in the winter, every day to oversee the project.
"Along the way, he and his sons collected snakes, which, to the
consternation of visitors, he kept in his office. Sculptors used some of
Meigs's snakes as models for the Capitol's door rings and handles,"
wrote William Offutt in his history of Bethesda.

While work on the aqueduct officially began in 1853, work on the
bridge did not begin until 1857 when Congress appropriated the first
funds. Masons completed the stonework on the arch by July 1859.
Also that year, perhaps to encourage Congress's continuing interest
and support, Meigs put on a demonstration of his aqueduct pumping
valves for members of Congress. He sat on the wall of a fountain on
Capitol Hill as water shot 100 feet into the air. The project would
ultimately cost more than $2 million.

With the aqueduct bridge under construction during the Civil
War, Cabin John became the scene of Union troop encampment.

The bridge's wooden arch-ring support was removed in fear that the Confederate army would set fire to the bridge. Union soldiers camped near the bridge and the C&O Canal to protect them both.

Courtesy Richard Cook

Wagons crossed the Union Arch Bridge during the Civil War.

Chiseling Jeff Davis

When work on the bridge began, Virginia-born Jefferson Davis was Secretary of War. His name was on the bridge inscription but in 1862, after Davis had joined the Confederacy, Secretary of the Interior Caleb B. Smith ordered Jefferson Davis' name removed. A master stone-cutter named "John Babbinger," who was actually Joseph Bobinger, chiseled the name out of the stone, leaving the inscription on the bridge's western abutment facing south to read:

> Washington Aqueduct
> Begun A.D. 1853 President of the U.S.,
> Franklin Pierce. Secretary of War,
> _____, Building A.D., 1861,
> President of the U.S., Abraham Lincoln
> Secretary of War, Simon Cameron

On September 8, 1892, William R. Hutton, formerly one of the engineers, wrote to *The Washington Star* about how the name was removed. He recalled accompanying Secretary Smith and a few members of Congress on an inspection of the aqueduct.

"Turning to me the Secretary said: 'The first order I give you is to cut Jeff Davis' name off the bridge.' Not taking seriously the Secretary's remarks, I did nothing in the matter. A week later Mr. Robert McIntyre, the contractor, arrived to resume his work upon the bridge, and called to pay his respects to the Secretary. The Secretary said to him that they had put Jeff Davis' name on the bridge, and he wished they would cut it off. 'With the greatest pleasure, Mr. Secretary,' was the reply, and the contractor's first work was to remove Mr. Davis' name."

Capt. D. D. Gaillard of the Army Corps of Engineers wrote in 1897, "If forgetfulness of the bare historical fact as to who was Secretary of War at the time was the object sought by the erasure, the result has been a woeful failure, for the inherent curiosity of mankind is such that the erased name is more strongly impressed upon the memory of the visitor than would have been the case had it remained untouched."

Jefferson Davis' name was reinstated in 1909, by order of

Below: An empty space remained where Jefferson Davis' name had been removed from the Union Arch Bridge.

Right: J. B. Horne restored Jefferson Davis' name to the bridge.

Courtesy Richard Cook

Courtesy Richard Cook

57

President Theodore Roosevelt, after a two-year campaign by women of the Confederate Southern Memorial Association led by President Mrs. Katie Walker Behan of New Orleans, Louisiana. The tablet with the inscription was five feet high and 11 feet long. Over 750 pounds of rock to a depth of one inch had to be removed and recut to restore the name.

Courtesy Richard Hirsh

J. B. Horne displayed his stone cutting tools.

The stonecutter who restored the name, J. B. Horne, from Moss Point, Mississippi, had read as a boy about removal of the name during the Civil War and had long wanted to be the one to put it back. He bid for the job and was hired. He used 24 chisels and a hammer to complete the restoration. After completing the job, he sold the tools to Mrs. Behan for $50. She had the tools placed in the Jefferson Davis repository at Memorial Hall in New Orleans.

Another erasure of less-prominent figures had also occurred earlier at the bridge. During an absence of Meigs, two engineers in charge of the project for a short period had their names cut on two arch stones near the east abutment, immediately under that of Meigs, designating themselves as "Chief Engineers." When he returned, seeing what had been done, Meigs ordered the names erased since the work performed by them during his absence was simply a continuation of his projects and plans. Blank stones remain where the names were erased. The inscription now reads:

> M.C. MEIGS
> Chief Engineer
> Washington Aqueduct
> A.D. 1858
> Fecit

On the east abutment, the inscription reads:
UNION ARCH
Chief Engineer, Capt. Montgomery
C. Meigs, U. S. Corps of Engineers
Esto Perpetua

Romantic Destination

Many photographs and postcards during the late 19th and early 20th centuries brought romantic images of the arch over Cabin John Valley to the homes of thousands of visitors. On December 29, 1889, the Washington Post reported a Christmas picnic party at Cabin John Bridge where a group, wrapped in robes, had "a genuine summer picnic down under the great arch of the wonderful bridge, the largest stone arch in the world, with the luncheon spread on a broad rock."

Courtesy Richard Cook

Above: A wooden staircase led to Cabin John Creek ca. 1900.

Right: The Capital Bicycle Club posed at the edge of Cabin John Creek under the Union Arch Bridge in 1883.

Columbia Historical Society; courtesy Reed Martin

Another article in 1886 described a bicyclist crossing the Cabin John Bridge riding the three-foot high stone parapet instead of the roadway. That feat was said to be repeated by a number of teen-agers even in the 1950s before the parapet was shielded by fencing. Many stories were told over the years of Cabin John children walking on the parapet.

In 1910, in a cold winter, the conduit suffered a crack for the first time and water froze as it leaked over the bridge. The cascade of frozen ice is seen in news photographs and repair became the topic of hearings before Congress which authorized $35,000 for repairs.

Courtesy Richard Cook

Water froze as it leaked over the bridge from a crack in the conduit during the cold winter of 1910.

Guards were stationed night and day at Cabin John Bridge in May 1924 to prevent anyone from entering or leaving Cabin John. The entire area of Cabin John to Potomac, Md., had been quarantined because eight cases of smallpox had been found in a lumber camp near Great Falls. Only those with a vaccination certificate were allowed to travel, and Cabin John residents without one were ordered to stay home or submit to vaccination.

Second Aqueduct

In 1926, an additional ten-foot diameter conduit was constructed along Conduit Road to increase the water supply for Washington by 100 million gallons a day. During construction, the majestic cedars that lined the road from the bridge were cut down, destroying one of the beautiful features of the landscape, much to the dismay of residents. The Army Corps of Engineers raised Conduit Road about six feet to hold the aqueduct, leaving many front yards and homes below the level of the road.

Resident Presley Wedding had childhood memories of the construction of the second conduit, as described in Offutt's book *Bethesda*. "It came right through our front yard. The steam shovels used to wake us up in the morning. They left manholes for access and built it all the way down to Cabin John Creek...Fortunately they left ladders out there so we'd climb down through a manhole and walk all the way through the conduit till it came out at the creek on the way to school."

According to Offutt, the Corps of Engineers ran the second pipe into the Cabin John gorge. The two aqueducts are interconnected in three places to permit repairs without cutting water service.

The Washington Aqueduct still supplies the nation's capital and parts of nearby Virginia counties with public water, carrying more than 185 million gallons each day. Montgomery County, Maryland, including Cabin John, receives not a drop of the water flowing through the aqueduct, even though it is largely within its domain. Cabin John's water comes from a separate purifying and distribution system operated by Washington Suburban Sanitary Commission and starting from the Potomac River above Great Falls. One of WSSC's water towers stands at 6711 Tomlinson Terrace. The elevated tank went into service on New Years Day in 1946 with a capacity of 500,000 gallons. Every day the tank releases water into the system and every night water is pumped back into the tank.

Bridge Traffic

The narrow Union Arch Bridge carried two-way traffic for more than 100 years. In 1863, when the bridge was completed, only small ankle-high timbers lined the edges. It was not until 1872, as traffic

Montgomery County Historical Society

In the 1940s, two-way traffic on the bridge brought trucks, pedestrians, and children on bikes too close for comfort.

61

increased on the road and the bridge, that a parapet of red sandstone was added. In the mid-1970s, metal fencing was also added.

In the 1950s, the Cabin John community became concerned that pedestrian and bicycle traffic had little access with traffic on the bridge. Even as late as 1970, Richard Cook recalled, as a newly-licensed young driver, having to back up off the bridge in his parents' 1967 wide-body Pontiac because he met and couldn't pass an equally wide-body Cadillac DeVille coming from the opposite direction. A pedestrian section was finally added in the mid-1970s and the bridge became one-lane for vehicles.

Courtesy Tim Weedlun

One of many Cabin John T-shirts with a bridge design.

Over the years, residents of Cabin John have had a love and hate relationship with the bridge. The graceful beauty of the structure and its history have made the bridge a Cabin John icon. The Interior Department designated the bridge as a National Historic Landmark in 1973. Drawings of the bridge arch have been used on Cabin John T-shirts. Old photos grace *The Village News* and history panels displayed at the community center.

Tim Shank

A stop light times one-way traffic crossing the bridge today.

But increasing traffic occasionally creates gridlock at the stop lights on either side of the bridge and periodic need for repairs to the surface and stonework have caused closures. In 2001, the bridge closing for four months led the Army Corps of Engineers and the Citizens Association to arrange for shuttle services to take bus-riders to alternate routes.

In the winter of 1974, a 700-pound section of the ledge projecting from the bridge crashed to the

Cabin John Parkway below. No one was injured but the bridge was immediately closed to car and truck traffic. Only pedestrians and bicycles were allowed from 6:00 a.m. to 9:00 p.m. The bridge remained closed to vehicles for more than one year until the Army Corps of Engineers released its report, "Restoration of Cabin John Aqueduct Bridge," in January 1976.

Montgomery County Historical Society

In 1974, part of the bridge's ledge fell onto the parkway below. No one was hurt, but the bridge remained closed for nearly two years during repairs.

The report concluded that the bridge was passable except for some surface deterioration and removal of the projecting ledge. The Corps proposed three "schemes" for repairing the bridge. Scheme 1 would require closing the bridge to all but pedestrians, bicycles and emergency vehicles at a cost of $749,000; Scheme 2 would permit pedestrians, bicycles, and vehicular traffic under six tons and cost of $731,000; Scheme 3 would allow only pedestrians and bicycles and cost $583,000.

The report was presented at a Cabin John Citizens Association meeting where residents, frustrated by the bridge closure for more than a year, demanded that the bridge be reopened immediately, even on a temporary basis, since it was structurally sound. Instead, Harry Ways, the Corps representative, said he would recommend further study to reopen the bridge.

Angry citizens went on to discuss seeking legal advice and considered filing suit for damages to get the bridge reopened. To gain attention from the Corps and anyone who could help, residents even staged a demonstration at the bridge. Finally, with the help of Congressman Gilbert Gude (R-Md.), the bridge reopened to great fanfare on December 4, 1976. The cost of repair was $80,000, far less than original estimates.

Some 300 residents came out to celebrate. It was a very chilly day which prompted Rev. Allyn Rieke to comment, "They said it would be a cold day in Hell before we got the bridge reopened, and I guess they were right."

On the speaker's platform were officials from the Army Corps of Engineers and representatives of the Montgomery County Council, Maryland Department of Transportation, Maryland Historic Trust, Washington Suburban Sanitary Commission, and Cabin John and Glen Echo citizens associations. Rep. Gude cut the ribbon to reopen the bridge, and television cameras from two stations were on hand to record the event. Minda Wetzel, Cabin John Citizens Association Union Arch Committee Chairman, drove the lead car across the bridge followed by a fire engine from the Volunteer Fire Department, members of the 1st North-South Brigade from Alexandria in full Civil War regalia, officials, and Cabin John and Glen Echo residents.

The Brigade marched across with flags flying, reminiscent of Union troops crossing the bridge more than a century earlier.

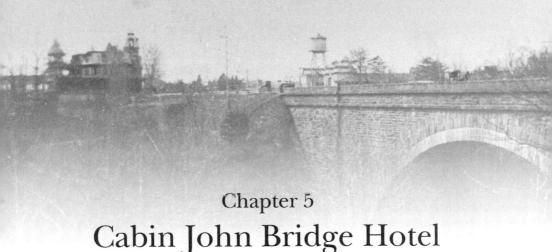

Chapter 5
Cabin John Bridge Hotel

"CABIN JOHN BRIDGE HOUSE, situated at Cabin John Bridge, about 7 miles from Washington, can be reached by a delightful drive over a splendid road. It is adjacent to the Potomac River, where there is the finest bass fishing. The house is cool and airy, some distance above the level of the river. A fine ballroom is at the disposal of guests and picnic parties will find fishing tackle for their use at reasonable rates. The bar is stocked with the choicest liquors, at city prices. Boarders are accommodated by the day, week, or month at reasonable rates. Joseph Bobinger, Prop'r"

What began as a refreshment stand for workers on the conduit and bridge became a sumptuous establishment frequented by the most powerful politicians and important social figures of Washington, D.C. The story of the hotel is like a story of America, beginning with an immigrant who rose to importance and a population seeking new destinations for adventure.

One of the stone masons who labored on the bridge was Joseph Bobinger. Joseph was born in Germany and emigrated to New York in 1854. According to the family's history, he was headwaiter of a hotel in Philadelphia for several years before coming to this area. Registering as a stone mason, he was informed that workmen were needed in Maryland. Work had already begun on the bridge when he arrived with his wife Rosa.

Courtesy Richard Cook
Rosa Bobinger.

While Joseph found work at the bridge, Rosa started a refreshment stand next to the bridge for the hungry workmen. She also sold cigars, snuff, candles, cold drinks and pies. Later, she and her husband leased and renovated an old construction shed for their growing business. It turned into a boarding house with a few rooms for workmen. Her reputation spread as she began to serve chicken dinners to Army engineers and laborers.

As business grew, the Bobingers needed bigger facilities. In 1870, with a loan from Riggs Bank, they bought 100 acres of land and built the central part of their hotel. Modeled after a German tavern, it was painted creamy yellow and had 25 rooms. The Bobingers called it the Cabin John Bridge Hotel.

Courtesy Richard Cook

The front of the Cabin John Bridge Hotel faced Conduit Road.

It was the food and drink at the hotel that kept the crowds coming to Cabin John. A regular dinner cost $1, and Rosa's "Chicken a la Maryland" was a signature meal made from her favorite recipe. She laid curled bacon strips over the top of each piece of chicken while it was fried "to keep it moist," as she said. Then she surrounded the chicken with heavy brown gravy and corn fritters.

Other special dinners included a small-mouth black bass split down the middle and garnished with tartar sauce and boiled new potatoes. Rosa's biscuits, made with buttermilk, were also famous. Wines were served, some made by William Reading who had vineyards on both sides of the Cabin John Creek. Every meal was served on cream-colored china with a brown floral border. Later, after Rosa's death, the hotel used Bavarian china decorated with the image of the Union Arch Bridge, surrounded by dogwood blossoms and marked "BB" for her sons, the Bobinger Brothers.

Hotel china at the turn of the century featured the bridge. The initials BB stood for Bobinger Brothers.

Courtesy Richard Cook

By the Creek were enclosures to keep Potomac black bass penned for later meals. A wooden footbridge under the stone bridge allowed visitors to walk closer to view the valley and the creek. The Bobingers also managed to get permission to construct an entranceway over the aqueduct north of the bridge and, wrote Offutt, "even more remarkably, to draw their water from the conduit itself and run it through their own purification system."

Joseph Bobinger worked on the Cabin John Bridge until its completion and was the mason who chiseled away Jefferson Davis's name after the Civil War began. He also became the first postmaster in Cabin John. The hotel was another example of his drive and sense of perfection.

In 1881, while having a heart attack, he walked off the hotel porch and fell to the ground, where he died. Rosa, left with two small boys, operated the hotel until her death from "a stomach ailment" in 1893. Both Joseph and Rosa Bobinger are buried in the cemetery yard of the Hermon

Tim Shank

Joseph Bobinger was born in Germany according to the 1870 census, but his gravestone cites France.

67

Presbyterian Church on Persimmon Tree Lane. The burial ground was not associated with the church when they were buried.

Resort Hotel Expands

Hotel operations were continued by their sons, George and William, who were the proprietors during its heyday in the 1890s and early 1900s. They stopped renting out rooms to overnight guests about 1900 and expanded dining. They remodeled the hotel in first-class style, adding two large banquet rooms. The hotel was so lavish and became so important as a destination for Washingtonians that the *Washington Post* reported about it regularly:

"If you should ask the first person you meet to tell you which suburban resort is the most popular, he would answer without the slightest hesitation 'Cabin John.' It is reached by the most beautiful drive from the city – over the Conduit road. The ride is just long enough to whet one's appetite, and the thought of a dinner at Cabin John Hotel is a pleasure that is only equaled by the dinner itself."

Courtesy Richard Cook

In this unique view, the Cabin John Bridge Hotel stood prominently at the end of the bridge ca. 1902. A water tower and carriage house stood across from the hotel.

Historian and author William Offutt wrote that the Cabin John Bridge Hotel was the most popular resort hotel ever operated in the Washington area and descriptions show why that was true. The lawns were filled with magnolias and flowering shrubs. Guests strolled down white stone paths to the rugged outcropping overlooking the canal and river. They could cross over the canal on the hotel's wooden

Fanciful illustration of the hotel.

Courtesy Richard Cook

"Lovers Lane Bridge" and descend to the towpath to walk or follow the many trails winding through the woods at the river's edge. When electricity became available, a thousand lights were strung up to illuminate the area from the hotel to the river.

Courtesy Richard Cook

Guests crossed a wooden "Lovers Lane Bridge" to reach the canal towpath from the hotel grounds.

Forty acres of shady lawns, fancy gazebos or summer houses, and elaborate gardens swept toward the C&O Canal and the Potomac River.

As the business prospered, the hotel's outbuildings multiplied with an ice house, smoke house, dairy buildings, poultry coops, stables, grooms' quarters, fish pens, gas house, and in the gardens even one of the largest asparagus beds in the country. Airy and casual summer houses, more like gazebos made mostly of

Courtesy Richard Cook

Gazebo "summer houses" dotted the hotel grounds.

cedar with open sides, dotted the gardens providing restful places for customers to sit and read or enjoy the natural surroundings.

Courtesy Richard Cook

The hotel had intimate dining rooms and larger public spaces.

When completed, the hotel had 40 guest rooms and two grand banquet halls, each with seating for a hundred. There were private dining rooms, two parlors, two bars, a barber shop, and a pool hall.

On the back of the hotel was a huge, octagonal orchestrion, imported from Germany with stained glass panels above bevel-edged windows. It was like a giant organ, imitating the sounds of many orchestral instruments. The music from the electric and air-powered band organ could be heard throughout the grounds and elsewhere down the road in Cabin John.

The hotel employed 17 bartenders and 40 waiters. The headwaiter, who spoke seven languages and remembered all the notable guests by name, trained his staff to impeccable service. The hotel became the gathering

Left: An ornate gazebo stood near the orchestrion in 1900.

Below: The orchestrion made a striking extension to the rear of the hotel.

Courtesy Richard Cook

Courtesy Richard Cook

place of diplomats, cabinet members, congressmen and social leaders. Speaker Joe Cannon held all of his social functions there. Presidents Theodore Roosevelt, William Howard Taft, and Woodrow Wilson were among those who frequented the hotel for lunch.

A bill for a dinner for 24 people in 1903 shows such delicacies as Canape a la Russe, Oyster

Oysters, sweetbread, Potomac bass and potted grouse were among delicacies served at the hotel in 1903. Notice the prices on this bill for a large group.

Courtesy Alan Darby

Cocktail, Potted Grouse in champagne sauerkraut, Potomac Bass a la Golbert, Sweetbread a la Eugene, and Asparagus Polonaise, for a total of $110.85.

The Bobingers baked their own breads, operated their own laundry, and offered fine wines from their well-stocked cellar. In 1899, people were also able to telephone the hotel before they left the city, calling 1002, and the food would be ready when they arrived.

The hotel was mainly a summer place. The family and their workers lived in the third floor with green shutters outside. Joseph's

Courtesy Richard Cook

Hotel carriage house ca. 1910.

basement rathskeller, with slot machines, and Rosa's Maryland fried chicken had brought a steady stream of customers by horse, wagon, bicycle and foot, even before the trolley cars in 1896. The rathskeller had a rough reputation while, at the same time, the main restaurant served very high-class clientele, an interesting contrast.

Trolley Ride to Cabin John

The Bobingers gave 10 acres on the east side of Cabin John Creek for a trolley turn-around loop and station platform for hotel guests. The trolley ride became one of the most picturesque journeys in the area and a sought-after excursion. As *The New York Times* reported in 1903,

"The trolley car lines around Washington offer the visitor to the city, and the dweller in the Capital as well, a number of enjoyable trips which will wile away these warm summer evenings in a very agreeable manner. Among the most picturesque is the ride up to Cabin John Bridge...The bridge in itself is well worth making the trip to see, but it is not the only thing to interest the sightseer at the end of his ride. There is a carousel, a scenic railway, a superb hostelry, and all the varied attractions of the first-class city summer resort."

The #20 trolley later carried mail sacks for the Cabin John postmaster and took commuters to work in Washington. The line started at Union Station in Washington, came out Pennsylvania Avenue to Georgetown, and traveled over rickety wooden trestle bridges with glimpses of the Potomac River. There were open summer cars until the 1930s. Trolleys continued until 1960.

Courtesy Richard Cook
1930 trolley to the Cabin John Bridge turn-around from Washington, D.C.

With the trolley line came electricity, and the gas house which had manufactured the fuel for the hotel's gas lanterns was no longer used.

Music, Theater

The Bobingers built a high cast iron bridge over Cabin John Creek, lighted by 500 electric lights, that connected the trolley station to the hotel grounds. Looking back in the 1940s, Norman Tuohey remembered being four years old and walking across the iron bridge the Bobingers built for their customers.

Courtesy Richard Cook

Guests crossed an elaborate iron bridge to the hotel ca.1900.

"I remember the bridge so well because I remember going with my mother to catch the street car. We'd walk past the hotel and go across the foot bridge to catch the street car. The bridge was as high and as big as the Cabin John Bridge.

"The Bobingers and my family were great friends, and I'd be in and out of the hotel with my people..." and in his small child's view, "The ballroom dome was about like the dome of the Capitol. And it was inlaid with gold."

In the hotel's gardens, during a party for staff of the *Washington Post*, John Philip Sousa and his 21 smartly uniformed musicians introduced his "Washington Post March."

Further expansion came to the hotel and excitement to its patrons with the opening in 1900 of a new theater on the grounds. The *Washington Post* reported on the grand opening that occurred on July 23:

"The handsome little summer theater erected on the bank of the Potomac at Cabin John Bridge was formally dedicated last night with

CABIN JOHN BRIDGE

The Favorite Resort of the Washington Public

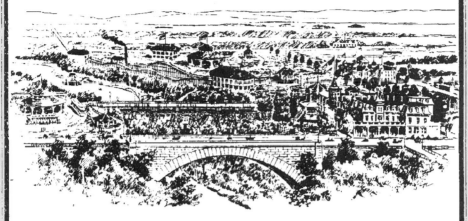

Always Cool---More Amusements Than Any Other Resort---Delightful Music.
Most Successful Season Ever Known.

A TRIP AROUND THE RESORT.

A ride out to Cabin John Bridge, either by street cars, along the Potomac, or by the smooth Aqueduct Road, is the favorite summer diversion of all Washingtonians. Here the air is always cool and invigorating, the scenery is beautiful and the opportunities for amusement are unsurpassed.

The Hotel at The Bridge is most attractive with its wide and cool verandas, overlooking the sloping green terraces and the many charms of landscape gardening as well as the bridge itself, unique in its great single arch, and the newer iron bridge, which is most in use by foot passengers. This hostelry is most famous, however, for its cuisine and excellent service. A New York chef is responsible for the well cooked menus this season, which have never been equaled at the hotel. Among the delicacies for which this hotel is well known are Potomac bass, and chicken, cooked Maryland style. Sunday morning breakfasts are popular this season, many coming out in their carriages or automobiles in the cool morning. These can be arranged for by 'Phoning Main 1002.

After dining at the hotel and listening to the excellent music of Haley's band, the visitor strolls down the pretty terraces and makes the round of the amusements.

Near the end of the bridge is the pop corn pagoda kept by Meixner Bros., of Baltimore. Almost everybody buys the delicious Korn Krispettes which look so tempting, and the attendants can hardly serve the public fast enough to keep up with the demand. The candy booth nearby, where fresh taffy is made while you wait, is always surrounded by people who like sweets. This taffy is made of pure sugar

and honey and if you buy one piece you'll come back for more. This booth is kept by C. S. Peters, who also has a lunch counter nearby.

You can't miss going up the broad and inviting entrance to the $30,000 scenic railway, owned by G. A. Dentzel, for this is one of the principal attractions at the bridge. A constant stream of people pour up the stairway to take the little cars for a whirl down the inclined railway and through the panoramic scenery representing the infernal regions, paradise, and other strangely illuminated scenes. The ride is thrilling, but perfectly safe.

On coming down from the scenic railroad you pause in the entrance for some of the excellent soda water served at the handsome fountain by C. F. Thompson and a corps of assistants.

Your next stop, around the circle of amusements is at the Merry-Go-Round, also owned by G. A. Dentzel, which is the finest and most expensive around Washington. Here the children have great fun, and so do the grown folks.

Just back of the Merry-Go-Round is the Amusement Palace kept by the genial and pleasant Geo. C. Waltham, who will let you "hit the babies" or the coon's head or try your hand at shooting at ingeniously arranged targets.

If you feel warm, drop into the building at the west side of the circle, where you can take a "trip to the Klondike."

Visit the enchanting Palm Garden by all means. This is an unusually attractive summer theater, where portrayals of intensely realistic Motion Pictures are shown nightly. These are out of the ordinary, absolutely true to life, and thrilling in many instances. In addition, there is provided excellent vocal and instrumental music and first-class novelties.

The best people go to Cabin John Bridge. Good order prevails and no objectionable characters are allowed on the grounds. A feature this year much appreciated by everybody are the fireworks and Haley's Great Band.

That it has been the biggest season on record at Cabin John, despite the bad weather, is partly due to the capable management, which is tireless in its efforts to provide wholesome amusement for the enormous crowds who visit the resort.

CABIN JOHN BRIDGE,
JOHN J. NOONAN, Manager.

An early 1900s advertisement depicted the scenic railway, carousel and grandeur of the Cabin John Bridge Hotel.

a vaudeville programme which compared favorably with the winter offerings in local vaudeville houses. The new theater, christened the Palm Garden because of the scheme of interior decorations resembling a conservatory, has a seating capacity of about 1,200, and it was almost filled last night with an audience anxious to be amused."

The building was located in the rear of the hotel, across from the scenic railway, and overlooked the Potomac River.

"The new theater is a very cozy and artistic affair," another *Washington Post* article observed. "The main entrance is brilliantly illuminated with electric lights and is decorated prettily with palms. Inside, the walls are painted in imitation of a conservatory, painted palms blending nicely with real palms ranged along the walls. The proscenium arch is broad and graceful...There is no balcony, but the main auditorium will comfortably hold over 1,200 people."

The plan was to have Saturday evening vaudeville and daily matinees for women and children at 4 p.m. However, managers of the theater appeared in court two months after the opening on charges they had violated the Sabbath by giving vaudeville matinees on Sunday. After that, mentions of the theater appeared in news reports for several years and then suddenly stopped.

William and his wife Mary ran the hotel until 1914 when he leased it to others to operate. He also leased some of the property to a large amusement company. In 1920, an amusement park opened on the grounds with a carousel, coaster rides, picnic area, dancing pavilion, and other attractions. Remarkably, according to research by Richard Cook, a Dentzel carousel with hand-carved wooden horses had been installed at the hotel as early as 1876, which would have been one of the earliest by the famous German wood carver Gustav Dentzel.

William was one of the first in the area to show motion pictures at his small amusement park, but business started to decline. The amusement area and the rathskeller brought rowdiness and fights, stabbings, and even several murders. The restrictions imposed by local prohibition laws and later by enforcement of Blue Laws cut deeply into the business. Modern attractions such as country clubs and a new amusement park with rides at Glen Echo began to draw customers away.

William died in 1926, and that year his widow padlocked the building, with everything in it including a hotel register with the signatures of ambassadors, politicians and presidents. She also set up a snack stand at the end of the trolley line on the opposite side of the Union Arch Bridge. Her sons, William and Harry Bobinger, began a taxi service to take people from the trolley to their homes across the bridge in Cabin John. They charged a quarter to Persimmon Tree Road.

Fire!

On April 7, 1931, the uninsured hotel burned to the ground, still full of its furniture and antiques, silver, china and glass. Cabin John resident Jerry Shaw was 11 years old when her mother woke her in the middle of the night to see the fire from the window. "The flames were wild-looking, even though we were blocks away. It had been in terrible shape for years and much of it had collapsed," she recalled years later.

Gone but not forgotten, the Cabin John Hotel had fame that lived on past World War II. In 1947, *Washington Post* cartoonist Richard Mansfield depicted the hotel, its dining and Palm Garden in a cartoon labeled "Those Were the Happy Days."

Historical Society of Washington, D.C.

In 1947, Washington Post cartoonist Dick Mansfield featured the Cabin John Hotel.

Because some of the china and silver were used to carry out food for guests, a few pieces continued in other hands. Some of it has appeared at antique shows and on eBay to the delight of collectors. The only remaining evidence of the hotel itself is the small brick gas house next to two tennis courts now at the western end of the bridge, and a portion of sidewalk on the other side of the road. In 1989, the gas house was designated a county historic site.

Tim Shank

The hotel's gas house remains today.

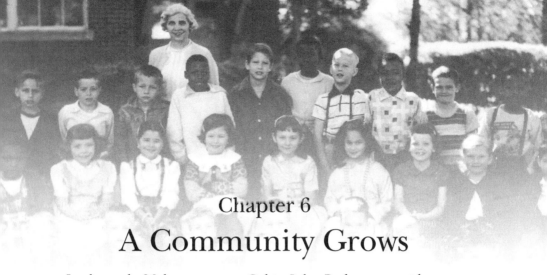

Chapter 6

A Community Grows

In the early 20th century, as Cabin John Park grew, residents became concerned about services for the community such as better mail delivery, street lighting and telephone lines. To work for improvements, a few interested citizens founded the Cabin John Park Citizens Association in 1919. Four of the active members became known as the Four Horsemen of Cabin John because they kept leading the charge to obtain needed services. They were Charles H. Godbold, Walter B. Armstrong, Ellis R. King and A. C. Wilkins. (See list of Citizens Association Presidents, p. 129)

Like Cabin John Park itself, the Citizens Association constitution restricted membership to white people and to property owners over sixteen years of age. Race restrictions no longer apply and only adults may vote at meetings.

Mr. Godbold's daughter, Josephine, recalled her father's work with the Citizens Association. "...the Citizens Association was really responsible for getting the roads and everything else going...in the twenties it was a very active group. Our roads were all dirt at one time. It was just a gradual process of them all working together, fighting for it, and getting it done. They had to get the county to do these things..."

In the fall of 1923, Armstrong, Association president, wrote a strong letter to the president of the C&P Telephone Company complaining about the phone service. At the time, 60 people shared four telephone lines. Three years later Mr. Armstrong wrote again, exasperated about an increase in telephone rates from $1.25 to $1.75 a month. He wrote:

"Another dissatisfaction with the overloaded rural lines is the manner in which the calls are handled. On my own line, for example, there are a couple of parties whose telephones are apparently seldom answered, and the operators for some reason unknown to me ring these phones for an hour at a time. This constant repetition of a ring 75 or 100 times at intervals all day long certainly is an annoyance to everyone else on the line, whose phones of course also ring. Then there are of course the many 'listeners' who interfere with your privacy and prevent the user from hearing distinctly."

C&P offered individual or four-party service to Cabin John residents in addition to the overloaded rural lines. The individual rate went as high as $11.75 a month.

It was not until 1932 that the Citizens Association appeared to be satisfied with a new "metropolitan" service that, while somewhat higher in cost, did not include a mileage charge or toll on calls into Washington.

Charles R. Smith was a charter member of the Citizens Association who didn't go to meetings very often. The first time he went, when he saw the strong opinions expressed, he said "This is a good place to either get blessed or cussed."

Meetings were held in Junior Hall, short for Junior Order of American Mechanics, which is today a large gray building that is both a home and office next to the MacArthur Plaza shopping center. For several years in the mid-1920s, Junior Hall was a community gathering place with meetings and social activities such as country dancing.

Tim Shank

Junior Hall, 2007.

In 1926, a trash-collecting service was set up, and 500 people attended a community fireworks celebration on the 4th of July.

The 1920s also saw the start of the Cabin John Home Demonstration Club. The club started the campaign for a new school and the Citizens Association took up the banner. The Club sponsored the first baby clinics held outside of the county seat, and in the 1930s sponsored a summer school for girls to learn sewing, health and cooking. By 1941 the membership extended over such a large area that the name was changed to Potomac Valley Homemakers Club.

The Cabin John Park Citizens Association sponsored its first Boy Scout troop – Troop 105 – in 1928 and the first Girl Scout troop in 1930. In 1935, David Armstrong, a Cabin John Eagle Scout, had the honor of being selected to present the five millionth copy of the Boy Scout Manual to President Franklin Roosevelt.

From the late 1950s through the 1970s, the Cabin John Citizens Association worked to preserve the sylvan environment and life style of the community, fending off mall-style commercial development. The Citizens Association continues to play a major role in furthering community values and preserving Cabin John's identity. Monthly meetings are held at Clara Barton Community Center, and CJCA helped lead the transformation of the building from a school to a multi-faceted activity center.

The Association also leads an annual clean-up of Cabin John Creek and cooperated with the county on improvement of Seven Locks Road and adding a bike and walking path on MacArthur Boulevard. It has joined in efforts to reduce noise and pollution from aircraft using Reagan National Airport and monitors all zoning issues affecting Cabin John. The Association sponsors many community and family-oriented social activities such as a holiday party in December, house tours, summer canoe trip on the Potomac River, community clean-up day, blood drives, July 4th parade and the annual Crab Feast.

The Crab Feast is the largest community event, held at the Clara Barton Community Center on the afternoon of the first Saturday after Labor Day. The Crab Feast draws hundreds of people of all ages, and dozens of volunteers contribute time to organizing and carrying out the event.

In 1967, a monthly community newspaper began publication with a modest mimeographed sheet. It didn't have a name when it first appeared and offered a prize of $1 "plus two pounds of Cabin John Sausage" from the Good and Quick shop for the best suggested name. Today, *The Village News* is a 12-16 page newsletter, professionally printed, and the major source of community information on activities, people, developments and "looking back" historical vignettes. Ads from local businesses and funds from the Citizen Association, raised through the Crab Feast, cover the printing and mailing costs.

All of the work – writing, editing, layout and design, business management and mailing – is done by volunteers. When Linda

Billings, one of the active volunteers on the editorial team and also a staunch environmentalist, died tragically in 1985, the Citizens Association established a memorial to her at the Union Arch Bridge. Among long-term volunteers, Andy Rice, former editor, has written a "Looking Back in Cabin John" column and Barbara Martin, former news editor, has written "Neighborly News" for dozens of years.

In 2007, a complete digital archive of 40 years of the newsletter was compiled by the editors and other volunteers who collected the issues. A few years earlier, the Citizens

"The Village News" was redesigned with a new look in 2004.

Tim Weedlun

Association also developed a Web page (*www.cabinjohn.org*) and began an occasional e-mail service to alert residents to meetings and important events. (See list of *The Village News* editors, p. 131.)

Fire Department

In 1930 Charles Benson led the community in establishing a fire department. The Cabin John Park Volunteer Fire Department was incorporated with ten charter members meeting at Benson's store.

The Tuohey family gave one-half acre of their land for the firehouse to be built at the corner of Conduit Road (MacArthur Boulevard) and Seven Locks Road. They once owned all the land that is now a shopping center. A blacksmith's shop was on the corner and Loretta Harrison Tuohey refused to make the blacksmith move, so the firehouse was set back behind his shop. The firehouse for Company #10 was built entirely by the volunteer labor of Cabin John residents and took two years to complete. The first meeting held at the new firehouse was in March, 1932.

The first fire truck was a Model T pick-up with a 100-gallon portable pump. Before the firehouse was built, it was stationed in

Courtesy Mary Morgal

Cabin John Park fire department had a dozen volunteers in 1933.

a shed at a resident's property on the corner of 77th Street and Conduit Road. Next the fire department bought a new Brockway 300-gallon-per-minute pumper with 400 feet of hose. In 1936, they obtained a Cadillac rescue wagon from Bethesda Fire Department to replace the Ford pick-up. Other pumpers used by fire departments in Washington, D.C., Takoma Park and Laytonsville found their way to Cabin John, often at bargain rates.

Courtesy Gerald Quinn

A 1935 Brockway, which still runs, was one of the first fire trucks for the Cabin John Park fire department. Chief David Tuohey stands on the right.

In 1938, a "Ripley's Believe It or Not" cartoon sketched the firehouse with the text, "The Fire Department Without Water. Although a million gallons an hour flow past the front door, and Cabin John, MD maintains a fully equipped fire department, the village has no water supply. Yet conduits supplying Washington, D.C. run directly in front of the firehouse."

Ripley's may not have known that the firemen would dig down a foot to get to manholes along Conduit Road so they could draft water out of the conduit. Loretta Tuohey Hall recalled "They gave us permission to go to those manholes." Or they would go to the canal or the creek to relay water, according to her brother Gordon Tuohey.

In the years after the firehouse was built, additions and remodeling converted the upstairs dance hall into offices and a bunk room. A recreation room was added to the first floor and then an ambulance bay.

Courtesy Mary Morgal

The firehouse in 1973.

In the 1930s, Glen Echo's volunteer fire department competed for fires with Cabin John, sometimes racing across Cabin John Bridge. During World War II, relations between the two fire departments improved.

Acrimony and dissension marked early years of the fire department. One of the firemen was charged with arson and two fire chiefs were removed for various allegations. Fire occurred mysteriously in abandoned houses, including the Cabin John Bridge Hotel. Dennis Tuohey and Alden A. Potter, father of future Montgomery County Executive Neal Potter, locked horns over whether the firehouse should include a beer parlor. Potter opposed the idea and ultimately resigned.

A local newspaper, the *Sentinel*, reported in the spring of 1931 that the fire department was "torn by internal dissension." At one point, the Cabin John fire board considered whether to ask all of the firemen to resign and start over. But by the fall, a reorganization took place that resolved some of the tension.

That first firehouse did not have a phone or electricity for an alarm. Mary Hook Morgal remembers as a teenager being asked to sit at Tuohey's Tavern to listen for the phone to ring in case there was a fire call. If such a call came, she would climb the narrow steps to the second floor to pull the switch that would trigger the siren on the roof of the firehouse.

"When I was a teenager I used to do some book work for David Tuohey. If the fire phone rang from behind the bar, I would run and get it, get the address, and then I'd climb the stairs to a storeroom where there was a light switch. You'd switch it up for the siren at the station to get to a high pitch and down and up again and down and up again, run down the steps and get to the firehouse and give whoever was there the address."

The sound of the siren was a familiar part of Cabin John life as it summoned volunteers from throughout the community.

Courtesy Mary Morgal

The Ladies Auxiliary, in beach pajamas, won the firehose hookup trophy in 1931.

There have been many fire chiefs, including several Tuoheys, and it was a Tuohey who founded the Ladies Auxiliary. In 1931, the Auxiliary women wore beach pajamas and competed in a firehose hookup contest against a team of women from the Gaithersburg fire station. The Cabin John ladies won the trophy. In the early days of World War II, the Ladies Auxiliary threw a Christmas party for 200 soldiers guarding Conduit Road and the aqueduct.

The fire department also participated in civil defense during the war. In 1942, an all night blackout was staged in the Washington area as a drill, including aircraft flying overhead as if about to attack. The only injury to occur during the drill happened in Cabin John. Fire Chief Kenneth Tuohey was struck in the head by a fire plug cover as a hose was being hooked up.

Mary Hook grew up and married D. Everett Morgal, who first played on the fire department baseball team and then became treasurer for the fire department. Mary volunteered with the Ladies Auxiliary in 1953 and later headed the Auxiliary for 40 years. She still helps with fundraising and was honored in 2006 with a treasured firehorn for her service. A handmade fire truck mailbox with the Cabin John Fire Department insignia marks the driveway of their home.

Tim Shank

Left: *A fire truck mailbox graces the Morgal home. Everett Morgal was the fire department's treasurer.*

Below: *Mary Morgal was awarded a treasured firehorn trophy for her 40 years of leadership in the Ladies Auxiliary.*

Judy Welles

For many years the fire hall was the scene of community meetings and social events. It also was the place where the fire department majorettes would practice.

Margaret and Charlie Lawrence started the firehouse majorettes with the help of Dottie Clark and Mary Morgal to involve their daughters and other girls in an activity. In 1960, for the first parade, the women sewed white fur around little red skirts and bought white boots for the girls. Mothers would walk along the side as the youngsters marched. As Mary recalls, " If any of them wandered away to a carnival or something, we would bring them all back into the firehouse and iron everything out when we got them back there."

"There were 27 girls and they had white tops and bottoms with red sequin trim. In Clinton, Maryland, it rained and the red sequins ran all over the uniforms. I put the uniforms in a bathtub with Diaper Pure. The next day Mrs. Worsham [her neighbor] called me and asked, 'Why do you have all those little white panties hanging outside on the line?'"

Even in the 1960s, the short skirts proved to be a problem when the minister told the girls it was a disgrace for them to march down the street showing their arms and legs.

Parades ended in Cabin John when the heavier fire trucks were no longer allowed on MacArthur Boulevard. The majorettes continued to

Courtesy Mary Morgal

In the 1960s, Cabin John girls in "The CJs" majorettes twirled batons in holiday parades.

practice in Cabin John and participate in parades in other parts of the county until the late 1960s.

Originally staffed only by volunteers, the department added some county firefighters in 1959. Still, fire chiefs have always been volunteer firefighters. (See list of volunteer fire chiefs, p. 130.)

The fire department was a noteworthy source of heroes and hooligans. One time the fire chief was caught filling a swimming pool with water from the conduit and another time a volunteer was accused of setting a half-dozen fires. Indeed, in 1973, the department chose as chief a young man who had been convicted of arson.

Initially, Cabin John Fire Station #10 served adjacent Potomac as well as Cabin John. Growth of the population in Potomac prompted the Cabin John Park Volunteer Fire Department in 1967 to put an engine in service in a garage on River Road in Potomac Village, the present site of a veterinary hospital. The fire department established a sub-station, Station #30, on Falls Road in 1970.

Needing to expand with more equipment to serve the community, the fire department sold the firehouse in 1984 and moved the station to River Road near Seven Locks Road.

Tim Shank

Left: The converted firehouse today houses an architectural firm and a cleaners.

Below: The Cabin John Park Volunteer Fire Department built a modern firehouse on River Road near Seven Locks Road.

Tim Shank

The cornerstone marker of the original Cabin John building is now at the River Road station.

Volunteers fought fires and did river rescues in 1973 as they do today.

Today, in addition to fighting fires, the Cabin John fire department provides emergency medical services and handles rescue work on the Potomac River. The RRATS – River Rescue and Tactical Services Team – are responsible for rescue and recovery operations on the Potomac River and C&O Canal from the Washington, D.C., line to Seneca. And every year, just before Christmas, a volunteer firefighter dresses as Santa Claus and rides through Cabin John on a big red fire truck with siren blaring.

World War II

Between 1938 and 1942, the Civilian Conservation Corps begun by President Franklin Roosevelt actively worked in the Cabin John area. Some 160 to 180 CCC men, who lived in a camp at Carderock, worked with the National Park Service on repairs to the C&O Canal. They repaired the towpath, rebuilt bridges, and cleared and landscaped picnic areas as the Canal turned into a major recreational area. They did some renovation to a few lockhouses, including the one at Lock 10 in Cabin John. They also photographed and provided a historical record of the lockhouses, quarries, barns and stores that existed along the canal at that time.

During World War II, soldiers were stationed along Conduit Road at all the culverts, valves and access points to the huge water pipe below to prevent sabotage to the Washington water supply – just as Union soldiers had done nearly one hundred years earlier.

Cabin John took part in all civil defense precautions. Young teenagers became Air Raid Ward Messengers, trained to run through the streets when the siren blared to make sure lights were out in all of the houses. Among the Ward Messengers were Mary Hook, Herman and Bubby Worsham, Joan and Ray Bell and Marvin Barber. Later, civil defense also became an activity to engage some of the teenage boys who needed something better to do than ride roughshod through the community.

A number of Cabin John young men joined the military during the war, including two sons of Lew and Irene Worsham and both survived. The War Department reported in 1944 that Technical Sergeant James H. Wedding, son of Cabin John resident Harry Wedding, was a prisoner of war in Germany. A liberator bomber and flight engineer, he was recommended for an air medal.

A USO club was established at the Model Basin for servicemen. On June 4, 1944, it had a distinguished visitor during a waffle and sausage supper, First Lady Eleanor Roosevelt. To quote Offutt, "after supper the President's wife spoke briefly about post-war responsibilities and the exciting possibilities that lay ahead. She warned that all the world's problems would not be over at war's end."

VFW

The Cabin John Veterans of Foreign Wars Post 5633 was formed in 1967 with 97 charter members, 80 men and 17 women. Open to any veteran who served in a foreign conflict, the Cabin John Post met wherever they could at first, helped the sick and infirm in the community and provided flags for the 4th of July. In 1968, the Post bought two acres and a brick building near what is now the Great Falls entrance to the C&O Canal National Historical Park. The building was built in 1912 and VFW doubled its size, adding a meeting hall where members also held dinners such as the

Judy Welles

Neighbors gave Danny Harris "Honorary Mayor" status for his many good works in Cabin John.

90

annual oyster and bull roast. Pearman Marshall and Ralph Morgal were charter members of the Post. Among current members are Wayne Swisher and Danny Harris. Danny, the "honorary mayor" of Cabin John for all of the good work he has done for the community, has been responsible for obtaining American flags for Cabin John for many years. The flags continue to be mounted on telephone poles on MacArthur Boulevard for certain federal holidays. The flags remained up for an entire year after "9/11," the September 11, 2001, attack on the World Trade Center and the Pentagon.

Churches

Gibson Grove AME Zion Church, founded in 1898, was named after Sarah Gibson, a former slave from Virginia, whose family was one of the first families purchasing land on Seven Locks Road. A very spiritual person, Sarah gave a portion of her land for the church and in tribute to her generosity, members named the church after her.

Gibson Grove's first structure was a modest log cabin. It served as a church and also as a schoolhouse until Sarah had a one room school built near the church. At one time the church's grounds were used for burials, the last one in 1912, and Cabin John Creek was used for baptisms.

In 1923, Gibson Grove church was rebuilt on its present site, and over the years, more rooms, central heating, indoor restrooms, kitchen and dining rooms were added. A serious fire from a lightning strike occurred in 2005 with extensive damage, requiring new fundraising and hopes for repair.

When Sarah Gibson died in 1929 she was buried in a cemetery near the church and next to Moses Hall, a social center/school house/ meeting hall on Seven Locks Road for African Americans during the late 1800s to mid-1900s. Moses Hall served as a center for freed slaves from the Cabin John, Scotland, and surrounding area in Potomac to socialize with friends and families and provided support and caring. Also known as Morningstar Tabernacle Number 88, Ancient United Order of Sons and Daughters, Brothers and Sisters of Moses, Moses Hall was part of a larger network of lodges established by freed slaves throughout the metropolitan area. Dues were used to help those in need and support families when wage earners were sick or died.

The two-story structure of Moses Hall has disappeared but a cemetery remains. Diane Leatherman, a memorable past leader and volunteer in Cabin John, led efforts to enlist county support to preserve the cemetery. In 2007, the Cabin John Citizens Association dedicated an outdoor exhibit panel of historic interest about Moses Hall, the related cemetery and the Gibson Grove church,

Liz Gray

In 2007, the Cabin John Citizens Association developed an exhibit panel about Moses Hall school and cemetery. At the dedication were descendants, volunteers, and dignitaries. Left to right: Warren Fleming, Judy and Edgar Bankhead, Montgomery County Councilman Roger Berliner, Colleen and Trav Daniel with daughter Marley, Maryland Delegate Bill Bronrott, and Citizens Association President Burr Gray.

developed in part from a grant by the Montgomery County Historic Preservation Commission. Clearing of a path and some of the ground of the cemetery was accomplished by Boy Scout Troop 233 and Cub Scout Pack 1320. More effort remains to fully reestablish the Moses Hall cemetery.

The Hermon Church on Persimmon Tree Lane drew many members from the Cabin John community and was an outgrowth of Captain John's Presbyterian Church in Potomac, which was known in colonial times as Captain John's Section. The first services for the Presbyterians were held in 1725 at Captain John's Meeting House, a log

Tim Shank

Hermon Church.

Judy Welles

In 1926, the G. W. Shaler Memorial Methodist Episcopal Church in Cabin John had a bell tower. While no longer in use, the church bell has been preserved.

structure. As the congregation grew and scattered, members of the church formed other churches. For one of those branches, Thomas Dowling gave a three-quarter acre lot on which the Hermon Church was erected in 1874.

In 1909, Rev. Dr. G. S. Duncan, pastor at that time, laid out a burying ground in the rear of the church called the Dowling Memorial Cemetery. This was where the Bobingers were already interred.

Early church services for Methodists in Cabin John Park were held at the home of Charles Benson. In 1920, the Methodist congregation worshipped in a tent under an elm tree at the foot of what was then 5th Street. Funds were raised and in 1921, the G. W. Shaler Memorial Methodist Episcopal Church was built. The church was named for Dr. G. W. Shaler, a retired minister and "Bible man' living in Philadelphia, Pa., who had given continuous small donations totaling $250. The District Superintendent of Methodist Churches suggested that "out of courtesy" the church should bear his name.

Ralph Springmann remembered church socials. He told Elizabeth Kytle, "They would have cake sales at the church and ham and chicken dinners. They'd serve these dinners at tables at the

Tim Shank

Cabin John United Methodist Church.

Methodist Church....The church would give little entertainments with local talent; people would give recitations and all. And we all used to enjoy it."

The church has become the Cabin John United Methodist Church with separate services in English and Chinese.

The Full Gospel Washington Church, Assemblies of God, a 250-member congregation, moved to Cabin John from Washington, D.C., in 1986. All services were conducted in the Korean language with interpretation provided. When the congregation moved back to Washington, the building on 78th Street began to serve the St. George Coptic Orthodox Church.

Tim Shank

St. George Coptic Orthodox Church.

In 2001, Adat Shalom Reconstructionist Congregation established a new building on Persimmon Tree Lane next to the Hermon Church.

Schools

The first school that served the area had one room and was built of logs. It was a short distance away on Persimmon Tree Road. In 1867, John Saunders, J. D. W. Moore, William Reading and Charles Dodge, "feeling the need to establish a good school in the neighborhood," bought an acre of ground not useful for farming from William and Elizabeth Dowling for $5. It had been a burying place for the Irish workmen who worked on the C&O Canal and died at the time of the cholera plague. The four men were the first trustees of the school, setting the teacher's salary and determining rates of tuition.

In 1884, the log school was replaced by a one-room frame building on the hill above the school. It was known as Friendship School and closed in 1914.

Friendship School.

Courtesy Gerald Quinn

Norman Tuohey attended Friendship School in 1912 when he was six years old. He remembered older children in the same room with him, up to the sixth or seventh grade. Some of the children in the eighth grade were 17 or 18 because they were farm boys who could only attend school for three or four months in the winter and kept returning to finish the grade.

He recalled, "There'd be only three or four in each grade. There was a bench up side of [the teacher's] desk; so when she held a first-grade class, they'd go up and sit on the bench; the rest stayed in their seats and worked. When she got through with the first grade, she called the second grade up." When Friendship closed, Tuohey went to Glen Echo School.

Glen Echo School No. 7, originally a one-room school, was built in 1892 on Wilson Lane. It was later partitioned into three rooms and a cloak room.

In 1925, the Glen Echo School enrolled 91 students. One of the teachers was E. Guy Jewell who became the first principal at the Glen Echo-Cabin John School. He described the Wilson Lane school at a PTA meeting in 1957: "It had a pump outside from which well water was drawn and carried inside...Toilet facilities were of the common kind, two little buildings out back."

He remembered among his first students Neal Potter (later the county executive), who lived on a farm between Conduit Road and the canal. On Boy Scout hikes, Jewell said, "it was a joy to stop at Mrs. Potter's. She always had nice, cool milk and fresh gingerbread."

Up to that time, many elementary school children had attended school in Washington, D.C., but the city stopped the practice to restrict the schools to taxpayers' children. In 1926, more space was needed for Glen Echo School and a building that belonged to the United American Mechanics, across from Tuohey's store and quite a distance from the main schoolhouse, was rented for one class. Another room was rented in the Glen Echo Baptist Church. The principal would drive his Model T Ford among the three locations to oversee the class instruction.

For students, "Bus transportation was something to behold. We never knew when the thing would get there, or when it wouldn't. Bus drivers weren't paid very much," Jewell said.

Mrs. Charles Smith recalled that when her children first started school, they had to walk up Wilson Lane. "They couldn't ride the bus because we were just on the edge of a mile. The bus only picked up children who lived more than a mile from the school. And they had to walk across the [Cabin John] bridge.

"This narrow bridge down here...the youngsters didn't have much trouble getting across it, but at PTAs, a lot of time was taken up about putting a shelf out on the side, or putting a fence down the middle somehow to protect these youngsters. The youngsters didn't worry about that. They got up on that parapet and went right on across."

With enrollment increasing in the late 1920s, the need for a new school became urgent. Its location, however, became a divisive issue between Cabin John and Glen Echo, each community wanting the school to be located on its side of the Cabin John Bridge.

Reminiscing, Mr. Jewell said, "...all of the argument went on as to whether it would be up the road or down the road, oh man, the fights between Glen Echo and Cabin John in those days."

The debate raged before the Maryland State legislature

Tim Shank

The Cabin John and Glen Echo communities are close neighbors, connected by MacArthur Boulevard and the Cabin John Bridge.

where the assembly held up a bond issue for 16 Montgomery County school projects in an effort to settle the controversy. The *Washington Star* reported on April 3, 1927, that the Cabin John Park Citizens Association presented evidence to the state legislature that the school-age population was centered in Cabin John. The legislature then chose Cabin John as the site. Land for the school was purchased from Mrs. Mary Bobinger, owner of the Cabin John Bridge Hotel, for $15,000, and J. S. Tomlinson, who owned ten feet beyond the street, deeded the strip to Montgomery County.

Even before the site was chosen, the name of the new school became another heated issue. Cabin John residents refused to let the new school have the old name – the Glen Echo School. Glen Echo citizens were equally

Theodore Denell, son of the locktender at Lock 7 and father of Cabin John resident Tommy Denell, attended 7th grade at a school on Wilson Lane in 1913.

Courtesy Tommy Denell

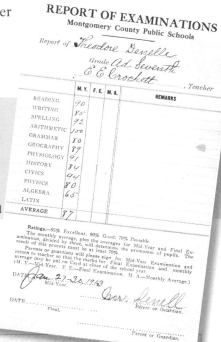

determined not to have it called The Cabin John School. The stalemate was resolved by agreeing to build the school on the Cabin John side of the bridge and giving Glen

Courtesy Gerald Quinn

Glen Echo-Cabin John School ca. 1928.

Echo top billing in the name, the Glen Echo-Cabin John School. A headline from 1928 reads, "Two Citizens' Bodies Plan to Co-Operate; Cabin John and Glen Echo Groups, Recently at Odds, Restore Amicable Relations."

In one of his "Looking Backward" columns in *The Village News*, Andy Rice wrote, "There was a joint meeting of the citizens of the two towns, a feature of which, according to a newspaper story, was a 'beauty contest in which men dressed in female attire.'" Some 15 national, state and community leaders were scheduled to make speeches at the dedication ceremonies in 1928 but fortunately only two actually showed up. Also in 1928, the Wilson Lane school closed when a new modern school was built.

The Glen Echo-Cabin John School was a one-story eight grade school with six classrooms, two of them in the partitioned auditorium. A small white building beside the school housed the kindergarten with steps down to a cafeteria. The school opened with 150 students and five teachers. Neal Potter was in the first graduating class. The school was a model of modern school design and earned architectural awards.

When the county allotment for the school didn't cover the cost of landscaping, Cabin John citizens donated bushes and flowers and worked on the grounds themselves. The Homemakers Club made curtains of dark red velvet for the school auditorium. David Tuohey got the material and his wife Mary supervised the sewing. PTA meetings began, and some of them in 1929 had such topics as "The Father As A Companion" and "Sex Education." A play with young Neal Potter as King Arthur was performed at one meeting.

A second story was added in 1930 when the school was made into an elementary and junior high school and the enrollment reached 330. The next year the ninth grade was transferred out of the school. By 1935, the school became a six grade elementary school.

The Maryland National Capital Park and Planning Commission completed plans in 1934 for a playground next to the school that would include two tennis courts, a clubhouse for Boy Scouts, handball and volleyball courts, small children's playground and picnic areas, and a baseball diamond and soccer field. Except for the clubhouse, handball and volleyball courts, that playground as originally designed exists today.

In 1944, the school's PTA recommended that the name of the school be changed to honor American Red Cross founder Clara Barton who had lived in Glen Echo in her later years.

A recreation center was built in 1957 beside the playground. Montgomery County hosted a variety of popular activities for

Tim Shank

Tennis courts, planned as early as 1934, were built near the brick gas house, a remnant of the Cabin John Bridge Hotel.

Cabin John youngsters including, in 1968, boys' flag football on Tuesdays and Thursdays, arts and crafts (for both girls and boys) on Wednesdays, and tumbling on Fridays after school – all for $1 each course. Activities continued until 1982 when the small recreation building was badly damaged by a fire which police suspected was an act of vandalism.

Despite high interest from the community for replacement of the building, costs made that less and less likely. In 1986, the Citizens Association began pushing the county to combine funding for a recreation center with planned renovation of the Clara Barton School. By 1990, funded by the county and also Cabin John, a wing of the building became the recreation center.

Cabin John got its first school for black children in 1880, known as Moore's School, a one-room schoolhouse located between River Road and Conduit Road. In 1911, the school was moved to Gibson Grove AME Zion Church on Seven Locks Road, which the Board of Education rented for a total of $7.72, and the name was changed to Cabin John Elementary School. The school was closed in 1922 because of low attendance, and for five years, 24 children were left without any school.

In 1926, a delegation of Cabin John parents appeared before the Board of Education to request a new school for black children. Instead, after several months, the Board rented Moses Hall and the children attended school there until 1931 when they were transferred to River Road School.

Above: Glen Echo-Cabin John School segregated class in 1954.

Below: Glen Echo-Cabin John School integrated class in 1955.

Both photos courtesy Gerald Quinn

When the U.S. Supreme Court ended school segregation in 1954, Clara Barton Elementary became one of the first schools in Montgomery County to integrate. The proportion of black students – 14 percent – was higher than in any other Montgomery County elementary school. Its PTA Integration Committee served as a model for other county schools, and integration occurred smoothly.

In the early 1950s, Mrs. Margaret Stein came to teach at Clara Barton for the next ten years. She was one of 16 teachers. She said, "Never before or since has my teaching given me so much satisfaction. The Cabin John children have respect and affection for their teachers. They have a close home unity. They are, more than any other group of children I have known, a pleasure to teach."

The enrollment at the school began to drop when Bannockburn Elementary School opened in 1957 near Glen Echo. By the late 1960s, Clara Barton Elementary's enrollment had become one of the smallest in the county with only eight teachers. In a hearing before the Board of Education on whether to keep the school open, citizens testified that the community needed to retain its "heart." Still, the Board voted to close the school at the end of 1974. The next fall, Cabin John's children were bused across the Union Arch Bridge to Bannockburn Elementary School.

The Clara Barton school building became Clara Barton Community Center, housing a day care center, recreation activities, and meetings of the Cabin John Citizens Association. How and whether to use the second floor of the school building continued to be a topic of concern for the Citizens Association. Even in 2007, citizens testified before the Montgomery County Council on the need for more storage and meeting room and space for an archive for Cabin John.

Courtesy Gerald Quinn

Clara Barton Community Center.

101

Cabin John's teenagers went to Walter Johnson High School and also Bethesda Chevy Chase High School until the mid-1960s when Walt Whitman High School was built. Pyle Middle School and Walt Whitman are among the most highly ranked schools in the nation with a diverse student population including many nationalities.

Post Office

Cabin John became a separate postal area around 1870 with Joseph Bobinger as postmaster and his famous hotel became the location for the post office. In 1890, another well-established Cabin John family became involved when Dennis Tuohey was named postmaster, a position he held for 35 years. The post office was located in his general store, basically where a post office now stands in the MacArthur Plaza shopping center. However, the post office moved around quite a bit in the intervening years.

J. S. Tomlinson; courtesy Richard Cook

Above: Cabin John Post Office in 1913, later Tuohey's Tavern.

Right: U.S. Post Office in Cabin John, 2007.

Tim Shank

Between 1925 and 1936, Mr. and Mrs. Charles Scott ran the Cabin John Post Office as part of the general store at 77th Street and Conduit Road, across from the Methodist Church. Wilbur and Irene Carper purchased the property from the Scotts and ran the general store and also the post office until 1942.

Ruth Tuohey Shuff, granddaughter of Dennis Tuohey, took over as postmaster until 1943 when she felt the hours were too much for her. Laura McKelvey assumed the position of postmaster from 1944 to 1972 and the post office was a small frame addition to her home on 77th Street. The zip code became 20731 and Shirley Shuler, a former Cabin John Gardens resident who had moved to Virginia, became postmaster in new quarters in one end of the Clara Barton School. The zip code changed to 20818 for Cabin John by 1982. LaVerne Baptist took over the position of postmaster in 1989 until her retirement in 2007. Jonathan Black became postmaster in 2008.

When Dennis Tuohey retired in 1924, the Cabin John Park Citizens Association appealed to the Post Office Department for better mail service. Mail was then received once every morning by a rural route carrier from the Bethesda Post Office who would also pick up outgoing mail. That meant that anything deposited at the Cabin John Post Office after mid-morning when the carrier departed didn't reach the Bethesda Post Office until late the next day and then it still had to be sent on to the Washington City Post Office for processing.

The Citizens Association suggested a faster system. They asked why the regular mailman working out of the Georgetown Post Office who delivered mail twice a day along Conduit Road to within a mile of Cabin John couldn't just continue on to deliver and pick up mail at the Cabin John Post Office? This request went unanswered. Today, mail is collected and dispatched three times a day from the Cabin John Post Office.

Commerce

The earliest industry in Cabin John was agriculture, with chickens, pigs and farm products brought to market by wagon along dirt roads.

The first mill of record on Captain John Creek, later known as Cabin John Creek, was patented in 1738. It was a flour mill called Mills Use on the Glen Echo side of the creek. But by 1803, a large stone flour mill called Cabin John Mills operated on the Cabin John side of the Creek.

The Cabin John mill was built on land called Doulls Park and ownership involved some of the most prominent businessmen of the area, such as Patrick Magruder and James Offutt. G. M. Hopkins' 1878 map shows "James Offutt's Mill Seat" where Seven Locks Road came to River Road.

Cabin John Mills manufactured some 40 to 70 barrels of flour daily in 1822, according to a notice in the "Rockville True American" newspaper. The mill house was 40 by 60 feet, three stories high, and "built of the very best materials." The notice for sale of half of the property added that there was also a "good miller house and some other small buildings on the mill seat. This is considered among the most valuable mill properties in the state of Maryland." This likely was the flour mill where the poem about John of the Cabin was found in a grain bin.

Courtesy Montgomery County Historical Society

Cabin John Mills, possibly in mid-1800s.

The mill suffered continuing financial problems and became known as "Magruders Folly." It went through several owners and was last operated as a paper mill before burning in 1857.

In the early 1900s, flour shipped by barge on the canal from a mill in Seneca. Dennis's grandson Norman Tuohey recalls:

"At Seneca they'd put the flour on a boat, the boat would come to that lock on the canal, they'd set the flour on the unloading dock for Cabin John and send word to the merchants. My grandfather used to get all his flour and corn meal and stuff there. Whoever tended the lock would send a kid or somebody to let him know it was there, and he'd hook up a horse and wagon and go on down there. And I'd go with him."

Between 1929 and 1943, the Bucolston Quarry located on the 24 acres between 80th Street, Caraway Street and Buxton Terrace, employed about a dozen men. It was owned by Hugh White, a federal government lawyer for the Commerce Department. The stone, of highest quality and beautifully colored, was used to build the Calvert Street Bridge in Washington, D.C., and also an underpass in Silver Spring, Md. The quarry closed because only small loads could be delivered. With the conduit underneath, MacArthur Boulevard had a two-ton limit for trucks, giving competing quarries on River Road an advantage. Also, Cabin John residents complained about the noise from blasting.

At least two blacksmiths operated in Cabin John. Judge Charles E. Benson – he was really a commissioner who could levy fines but didn't have a law degree – was a blacksmith on Conduit Road. In the 1920s, Jimmy Williams, who had worked for Benson, decided to build his own blacksmith's shop on the corner of Conduit and Seven Locks Road. When the firehouse was built, his shop stood next door. The blacksmiths were important for the canal mules as well as the carriage horses.

Judge Benson also had a store, a garage, a stable and a row of shed-like structures located where the Alpine Veterinary Hospital stands at the corner of Conduit and 78th Street. The store later became Cohens and then Sid's in the 1940s. A barbershop owned by Charlie and Ruth Tuohey Shuff operated next door.

Tim Shank

The Alpine Veterinarian Hospital stands today where Judge Benson's community store once was located.

Cabin John, which no longer has any gas station, once had two. In 1928, a gasoline and automobile accessory station was opened at the corner of Conduit Road and Tomlinson Avenue. In the 1950s,

105

Baker's store had food items and still had a gas pump. The Cohen family bought the store from the Baker family. Meanwhile, Sid's store a few blocks away had a gas pump too and a repair shop behind it, run by Walt Spates, serviced motorcycles in the 1950s.

In a series of sales and changes, Baker's then Cohen's store became a Sanitary market, Dickerson's Grocery, Good and Quick and, in the 1990s, Captain's Market.

LaVeta Fyock, who lived in Cabin John Gardens, where some of her children and grandchildren now live, recalled that Dickerson's Grocery still had one gas pump.

Tommy Denell said that in the 1950s, "In Cabin John, you could pick up a loaf of bread but there wasn't too much selection." Most people traveled out of Cabin John to Bethesda to shop.

Among the earliest businesses in Cabin John Park was Tuohey's store, with small groceries and general merchandise, which also housed the post office. The store became a gathering place. In 1917, William Case, who had been the proprietor of the Great Falls Tavern, built an eating place on the corner of Woodrow Avenue and Conduit Road (now 79th and MacArthur).

In 1932, David Tuohey applied for a license to sell beer and wine for on-premise consumption at the Wayside Store. At first his application was denied by the county but Tuohey appealed to the State Licensing Bureau. The Cabin John Citizens Association mounted a campaign against issuance of the license, generally opposing all efforts to commercialize Conduit Road since, in the words of a May meeting resolution, such establishments "carry with them a display of signs and resultant traffic congestion, etc., in the place of natural scenery."

However, other Cabin John residents supported the application and state authorities reversed the earlier decision and ordered that a Class "D" license be issued. What became Tuohey's Tavern and later Valley Inn continued for nearly 40 years.

During the 1940s, older children frequented a soda fountain after school at 78th Street, next door to Sid's store. The store closed and the soda fountain enlarged as frequenters came from other areas. Dana Swisher Lupton, Wayne Swisher's daughter, is one of many Cabin John residents with vivid and fond memories of the soda fountain. It was a gathering place that offered fun and friendship. But, after awhile, loud noise, some foul language and rough behavior started to disturb neighbors and church members across the street. In the late 1950s, the Methodist Church minister took some of the abusers to court and the soda fountain closed to become a laundromat.

When the soda fountain closed, Good and Quick became the place where teenagers and young adults hung out, often outside in the parking lot.

Captain's Market continues a long series of small food stores, with different names, in its location since the 1930s.

Tuohey's Tavern in Cabin John and Canada's in Glen Echo were frequented after work by some in Cabin John for a cold beer and light supper. "A lot of people gathered at Tuohey's beer joint. We never went, but older people did. I was on the police department and that was a beer tavern. I knew most of the people. At times it would get rowdy, but not usually," said Tommy Denell.

According to Toby Thompson, who wrote an article, "In Heaven there's

Taking a break on the back steps of Tuohey's Tavern were (left to right) Liz Hook, Node Embrey, waitress Gladys Coulter and cook Ms. Booth.

no beer, but heaven is not Cabin John," Tuohey's ran a tight ship in operating the restaurant and tavern during the 1960s. He did not tolerate rude behavior. But ill health led David Tuohey to sell the tavern. Under new management, the Valley Inn chapter of Tuohey's Tavern was rowdy and even dangerous, with fights and at least one stabbing. Business slacked off.

By 1974, the building stood vacant and vandalized, a hang-out for unruly juveniles. Condemned by the county, it was razed by the Cabin John Fire Department.

Courtesy Mary Morgal

Tearing down Tuohey's Tavern.

In the 1980s, a small shopping center called MacArthur Plaza was built between Seven Locks Road and 79th Street on property owned by the Tuohey family. The center included the post office, Market on the Boulevard delicatessen, Lucky Garden restaurant, and a bank. Later My Sushi restaurant joined the Plaza and the bank was replaced

Tim Shank

MacArthur Plaza shopping center was built where Tuohey's Tavern once stood.

by a video recording business and next by Salon Jean day spa. The Plaza also included some offices, a magazine publisher, and a knitting store at one point.

In 1983, the Bethesda Co-Op, a natural and organic food market, relocated from Bethesda to Cabin John and now has its own building in the rear of MacArthur Plaza.

A natural foods store, the Bethesda Co-Op relocated from Bethesda to Cabin John in 1983.

Two book publishers and a music publisher did business in Cabin John. Seven Locks Press, owned by Calvin Kytle and Andrew Rice, published books on politics and history; See-and-Know Press published He-ey-ey Lock by local writer and historian Morris Fradin. Cabin John Music Company published sheet music. In addition, members of what became The New Lost City Ramblers folk recording group met and practiced in Cabin John. They included Mike Seeger (son of Peter Seeger), Tracy Schwarz, Joan Cohen and Tom Paley.

Many businesses operate from people's homes in Cabin John including Mike Roark's MRBugs pest control, Ritch Kepler's picture framing, Robert Patch roofing, and John Rabner's painting and home improvement among others listed in the Cabin John phone directory.

In a *Village News* article in the 1970s about "brigadoon-like Cabin John," Fradin described a "pickle barrel beauty parlor." For many years, Dorothy Helen's Beauty Salon, at the corner of MacArthur and 78th where Level Fitness now resides, drew customers from a wide area. Women came to be "prettied up" and to buy honey, eggs, apples and also be served coffee, cookies and brownies while getting a hairdo. At one time aprons, doilies, napkins and other homemade products by members of the neighboring Methodist church were sold

Tim Shank

MacArthur Boulevard and Seven Locks Road is Cabin John's major intersection.

Tim Shank

for church fundraising. Pottery and oil paintings by local artists were also displayed for sale.

Public transportation has been an off-again on-again proposition in Cabin John. In the 1960s and early 70s, after the trolleys ceased, Glen Echo had a reliable bus service. Periodically, a bus would run along MacArthur Boulevard to the Good and Quick food market and back, but then it stopped. D.C. Transit Company gave the weight restrictions on MacArthur Boulevard as one reason for ending service. Citizens then argued for mini-buses that would travel to Persimmon Tree Road.

Between 1976 and 1985, there was no bus transportation in Cabin John until, with rising demands from residents tired of walking or driving to Glen Echo, Montgomery County began limited ride-on service. Currently, the small ride-on buses run during the morning rush-hours to Bethesda and return for the afternoon commute home. There is no bus service during mid-day.

Chautauqua '76

Cabin John held a gala Bicentennial Celebration, Chautauqua '76, on June 5, 1976. For the occasion, a booklet by Elizabeth Kytle,

Tim Shank

The home of Dorothy Helen's beauty parlor, a gathering place for the women of Cabin John for decades, became Level Fitness personal training and exercise.

Time Was: A Cabin John Memory Book, was published. It contained interviews with 18 "old-timers" documenting half a century of the early history of Cabin John.

A souvenir program "A Pride in Diversity" highlighted an extensive program of activity for the day along with short articles about Cabin John history, Cabin John Gardens and black schools in Cabin John.

Program cover from the 1976 Chautauqua celebration.

Courtesy Andy Rice

CHAUTAUQUA '76

THE BICENTENNIAL in
~cabin john~
June 5, 1976

· SOUVENIR PROGRAM ·

PLUS
A PRIDE IN DIVERSITY
3 PERSPECTIVES

ON

CABIN JOHN

THE NON-SUBURBAN SUBURB
~by Janet Dence and Morris Fradin~

THE STORY OF CABIN JOHN GARDENS
~by Dagny Newman~

BLACK SCHOOLS IN CABIN JOHN
~by Nina H. Clarke and Frank McKinney~

MAP BY JOYCE SEDGWICK
$1.25

The day began with a bike parade, batting contest and softball game between the Cabin John Volunteer Firemen and the Village News Volunteers. The afternoon saw mini-lectures by local historians Morris Fradin and Edith Armstrong, a play

111

about the C&O Canal, music of the Revolutionary era performed by the Cabin John String Quartet (Vera Dolezal, Louise Olson, Ellen Loeb, Andrew Rice), and an old-time gospel sing. There were also displays of Indian relics found in the area and silver and china from the Cabin John Bridge Hotel brought by Mrs. Harry (Mildred) Bobinger. The day ended with a community square dance on the Clara Barton School basketball court.

Opposite: Cabin John canoe "regatta" on Potomac River, 2007.
Katherine T. Andrle

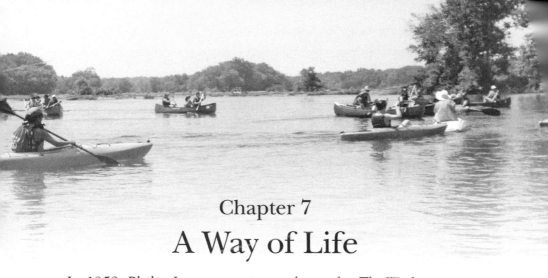

Chapter 7
A Way of Life

In 1959, Philip Love wrote in a column for *The Washington Star*, "In our swiftly moving age – and in an area south of Bethesda (where farm lands have been transformed into subdivisions, cows have given way to small pets, trees to lawns and paths to highways) – Cabin John Park still retains its quiet, bucolic charm...The residents are individualists: government employees, scientists, craftsmen, artists, writers, retirees, and nature lovers who value quiet, friendly and casual living – surrounded by woods and gardens – but within easy access to large population and trading centers."

How did these diverse people come to be in Cabin John and how has Cabin John managed to keep its "quiet charm?"

Beginning with Irish and other European immigrants, Cabin John has been a community where families continued to live for generations. Some of them came to farm. Others were workers on the C&O Canal. Some moved from the District of Columbia, first to summer houses and then to permanent homes. Later, in the 1940s, they came to work for the Navy's model basin and skilled machinists, metalworkers, carpenters and masons found their way from West Virginia and neighboring states.

Two generations of the Denell family, descendants of locktenders, continue to live in Cabin John. Six members of the Cable family have had their own families in Cabin John, four generations descended from one of the earliest residents, the Worshams. Four generations of the Fyock family have lived near each other in Cabin John Gardens.

In times past, Cabin Johners often hung out together and were involved in many activities in the community. So it was not unusual that marriages occurred between long-time Cabin John families. As an example, the Cables, Swishers, Peytons and Fyocks of Cabin John are closely connected through several generations.

Cabin John children, like young Douglas P. Cable, fished at the edge of the Potomac River where families tethered their boats. Flat bottom boats floated easily over the rocks for residents who wanted to fish in deeper stretches of the river.

Uva Mae Cable, daughter of Lewis and Irene Worsham, has lived 67 years in Cabin John and counts six of her 11 great-grandchildren also living in the community. Wayne Swisher, who has lived in Cabin John since 1942, is also grandfather and great-grandfather to the Cable clan because his daughter had been married to Uva's son. Another long-time Cabin John resident, Frances Peyton, is also related through a son's marriage to some of Uva's great-grandchildren. Uva's granddaughter Dawn Cable is married to Kevin Fyock, a third-generation Cabin John resident.

In 1939, Uva and her four brothers – Lewis ("Lew"), Virgil ("Buck"), Walter ("Herman") and Marvin ("Bubby") Worsham – moved with their parents to a Sears kit house in Cabin John. The house was built by the Reddens in the 1920s. She later moved with her husband and two children to a house in Cabin John Gardens, but returned to live in her parents' house in 1968.

The Worshams were a close-knit family. The Worsham parents also were charter members of the Glen Echo Baptist Church.

Uva's brothers caddied as teenagers at nearby golf courses including Congressional Country Club, Burning Tree and Kenwood. Lew, Buck and Herman grew up to be professional golfers and won tournaments. Bubby had a golfing scholarship to Wake Forest but

Courtesy Dawn Fyock

Above: The Cable/Swisher/Fyock family celebrated a graduation in 2007. (Left to right) Suzanne Cable, Darla Cable, Patrick Cable, Uva Cable, Kyle Fyock, Roger Lupton, Dana Swisher Cable Lupton (with Justin Cable in front), Evan Taylor, Wayne Swisher, Don Cable, Zachary Cable, Tyler Fyock, Dawn Cable Fyock, Kevin Fyock.

Left: Golfer Lew Worsham in 1940.

Courtesy Uva Cable

died in a car crash while a student. Lew won several major golf tournaments, including the U.S. Open in 1947 and the Tam O'Shanter in 1953 and was a member of the U. S. Ryder Cup team. He was also golf pro at Burning Tree.

Locktenders

Lockhouses still standing at Locks 8 and 10, accessible from Clara Barton Parkway, housed large families that were part of the Cabin John community. Solomon Drew was appointed the first locktender at Lock 8, given "use of the Lockhouse" for his family, land around it to garden, and a salary of $100 per year in 1830.

The lockhouse is an 18-foot by 30-foot stone structure, with two rooms on the first floor separated by a large central stone fireplace. Two more rooms are on the second floor separated by the fireplace chimney that rises through the ceiling and roof. The stone walls were once plastered on the interior, directly on masonry, and ceilings were lath and plaster which deteriorated over the years.

National Park Service

Lockhouse 8 had an enclosed back porch and neighbors on the canal – the Gates family – in 1938.

In 1915, Charles Spong was the last locktender at Lock 8, and twins Victor and Virgie Hall operated Locks 9 and 10, only a few hundred feet apart. Descendants of these locktenders lived in Cabin John until grandchildren became grandparents themselves.

Spong and his wife Sarah and three children lived in the lockhouse at Lock 8 where he tended the lock until canal operations ended. He was the ninth locktender to live in the lockhouse. One of his daughters, Myrtle Spong Fields, married John Fields and lived at the lockhouse where three of her children were born. For a time, seven people lived in the four-room lockhouse without running water.

One of those grandchildren born in the lockhouse in 1917 was Lillian Fields Stephens, who later moved to southern Maryland. A popular girl with many friends, she was called "Blyzz." She remembered her grandfather as a tall man, with dark hair, who always wore a "creased hat," like a fedora, even when he opened the lock. She and her brother Jack Fields, who moved to Texas, recalled that their grandfather had white geese in the front of the lockhouse.

Courtesy Jack Fields

Courtesy Jack Fields

Left: The lockkeeper's granddaughter, Lillian "Blyzz" Fields (center) with friends in 1940, was born in Lockhouse 8.

Right: Jack Fields at Lock 8 in 1940.

Myrtle and her growing family moved out of the lockhouse in 1920 (she had five more children), and her brother and wife moved in with their parents, the Spongs. The canal closed operations in 1924, but Charles continued to operate the lock for occasional pleasure boats.

Charles Spong and Cabin John are also related to one of the saddest stories of the C&O Canal. Samuel Spong, Charles' brother, was the canal boat captain whose three small children were scalded to death by a sudden burst of steam from a factory in Georgetown while they slept on the boat. The incident took place in 1916, just one year after Charles Spong became the locktender at Lock 8. He undoubtedly opened the lock for his brother to lock through on that fateful day.

Charles Spong died in 1934. He is buried in Potomac at the Methodist church graveyard on Falls Road. While not complete, payroll and other records of the C&O Canal Company identify many of the locktenders who opened and closed the Seven Locks during the years the canal barges locked through. (See list of locktenders for the Seven Locks, p. 128.)

In the 1930s, Myrtle and her children, including Lillian and Jack, lived in one of the houses at the top of the hill behind the lockhouse. The houses were later demolished to make room for the Clara Barton

Parkway. Lillian and Jack remembered the devastating flood of 1936 with water coming "half way up of the hill," pouring through the lockhouse windows, and reaching the second floor.

After Myrtle's husband, John Fields, died, she married Charles Muck, also a carpenter and friend of her husband. They moved back into the lockhouse in the 1940s, and Charles Muck repaired the back porch and installed running water from a spring behind the lockhouse. The Mucks lived in the lockhouse until the late 1950s.

During the early 1960s, a National Park Service ranger, Garland Williams, and his family, including daughter Susan, lived in the lockhouse for a few years. After 1963, the lockhouse remained unoccupied and boarded up, in a state of deterioration, until its restoration by the Potomac Conservancy began

Judy Welles

Charles Spong, the last locktender at Lock 8, is buried in the Methodist church cemetery in Potomac, Maryland. His daughter, Myrtle Spong Fields, and her husband, also are interred in that cemetery.

Courtesy Christine Gates Cerniglia

After her husband died, the locktender's daughter, Myrtle Spong Fields, married Charles Muck and lived in Lockhouse 8 during the 1940s. Mr. Muck added a screened front porch and rebuilt the back porch which had been damaged by the 1936 flood.

in 2001. Several founders – all kayakers – and board members of the Conservancy live in Cabin John. In 2005, the Conservancy's River Center at Lockhouse 8 opened to the public as a learning center on the canal and Potomac River.

River Story

The river has been both beautiful and brutal to Cabin John. The canal was built because the Potomac River was not navigable. In the disastrous flood of 1936, many people were left homeless. In that flood, one person was the kind of hero of which legends are made.

A woman was stranded on an island near Glen Echo as the river began raging. She got on the roof of her house with a board, a dog and a newspaper, and when the water rose higher, she moved to a tree next to the house with her dog. The water swept her house down the river. The Navy sent a boat with six sailors to rescue her but couldn't reach her.

The story goes on, as described by Offutt, "And here a couple of drunks from Cabin John were standing around and one says, 'I can get that gal off that tree.' And the other says, 'I'll bet you a case of beer you can't.' 'You've got a bet,' the first one says. He goes up to Cabin John where he's got this row boat, and he comes down through the trees rowing backwards... So he gets her off the tree, lots of people are watching now, and gets her into the rowboat, and the dog, and comes in to shore with all the people there...and the whole romance of this thing is she finally marries him."

The woman was Eva Dell Myers and the man who got her out of the tree and married her a year later was William E. Swainson, an accountant from Cabin John who had rowed on varsity crew at college. The storyteller failed to mention that Swainson came down the raging river with a younger man, John McCann.

Others remembered Bill Swainson as a squatter on the island near Lock 10 who lived there for at least 30 years. He built a bridge to get to his island and the pilings are still there. There are also abutments which indicate that at one time there was a vehicle bridge across the channel. As early as 1865 there was a road down to the river from Lock 10 and there were buildings between the canal and the river. An 1894 map shows a store to the right of the road, and on the left side was a house labeled "Swainson."

Buzzy Potter remembered that Swainson also kept goats, pigs and chickens on the island. He was a very strong and fearless man and people didn't cross him. In fact, he threatened to shoot people who wandered down his road. He was a legend himself and, in one version of the rescue story, he swam into the river during the flood and carried the woman back through the treacherous water.

Alcohol left its mark on Cabin John. Even one of the Bobingers was brought to court at various times for serving alcohol at the Cabin John Bridge Hotel on Sundays or during Prohibition. Tuohey's Tavern became a place of much carousing as beer was generously served. During Prohibition, at least two stills operated in Cabin John – one in the basement of a home and one in or near the lockhouse at Lock 8. "Bub" Spong, the lockkeeper's son, was said to be one of the distributors.

A family bought a house at a tax sale in Cabin John where the previous owner had been a moonshiner and bootlegger with a still in the basement. They had to put in a new concrete floor and drain because the smell of mash permeated the house in damp weather. They also got some late night knocks at the door by previous customers.

Offutt wrote that the word "drunk" was often lightly used "when men from Glen Echo and Cabin John talked about each other" in the 1940s. They also took pride in being called "river rats."

River Rats

Cabin John boys had a reputation as troublemakers in the late 1940s and into the 1950s, although it was sometimes hard to tell if it was simply rivalry with boys in Glen Echo. In one incident at the Glen Echo Park Crystal Pool, a group of Cabin John boys went into the pool at 7 o'clock on a hot summer evening. Bill Lehr recalled, "There

Teenagers, sometimes called "river rats," hung out at the Good & Quick store, later renamed Captain's Market.

Courtesy Tim Weedlun

might have been a hundred people in the pool and in a half hour we were the only people in that pool—suddenly. They would harass these people until they left. I watched in awe, bumping people, dunking them. They were bad asses sometimes, tough kids."

Mary Morgal said, "They had a lot of trouble with kids coming from other neighborhoods and causing problems in the 1950s. Kids in Cabin John all stuck together. I remember going to an Auxiliary county meeting and a woman mentioned an incident and said 'those hoodlums in Cabin John.' I said I'm from Cabin John and proud of it. If your kids had stayed in Kensington where they belonged, this would never have happened."

As early as the 1940s, the term "river rats" was used by outsiders sometimes to refer to people living in Cabin John Gardens and other times simply to talk about Cabin John. Naomi Denell recalled that "teenagers hung out at the Good & Quick store," later known as Captain's Market, and they were called "river rats."

As one outlet for some of the youths during the early 1950s, the Cabin John Citizens Association organized a civil defense squad that met weekly for training and drills. Several of the boys had raced motorcycles along MacArthur Boulevard, sometimes heard during Sunday services at the Methodist Church. It was no surprise that the minister – Rev. Dennis Chandler – became instrumental in leading the newly formed civil defense squad.

The motorcyclists soon became a special unit riding in the July 4th parades behind the fire department majorettes. Wayne Swisher said the motorcycle riders liked to test their racing skills on a dirt track near the Hermon Church, in the triangle between Persimmon Tree Road and Persimmon Tree Lane. The dirt road that later became Eggert Road was another racing road and also a late night lovers lane for teenagers in the 1950s and 60s.

"The motorcyclists had to stay away from the 'gulley guards,'" said Mr. Swisher, remembering the aqueduct police who would patrol MacArthur Boulevard for speeders and heavy load trucks. The motorcyclists repaired their cycles at Myers Garage, the building behind Billie Myers' home on MacArthur Boulevard, where they put a sign, "Dog Patch Speed Shop."

The term "river rats" stuck with Cabin John youngsters for close to half a century. In more recent years, it has come to signify the young Cabin John kayakers and canoeists who live close to and enjoy the river.

A third generation Cabin Johner, Maureen Willoughby remembers life in Cabin John in the 1960s when it felt like a small town with many different kinds of people. She also remembers feeling isolated from other nearby areas such as Bethesda because of a kind of discrimination over the countrified ways of Cabin John. In part because of Cabin John's reputation, her parents sent her to private school. Still, years later after marrying David Murphy, a park service ranger, Maureen opted to stay in Cabin John because of its calm, accepting ways.

In 2008, Maureen and David's youngest daughter Olivia, 14 years of age and the fourth generation in Cabin John, said she is glad to live in a small, safe place where she doesn't have to worry about crime. Like her mother's childhood memories, Olivia relishes living near the river. "When the river's low, you can walk on the rocks across to Virginia. And I even skate on the canal," she recounted.

People

Cabin John has always been a community of volunteers, whether for the Citizens Association, the fire department, the Crab Feast and other communal activities, or for protection of the river, the canal and the environment. In 2008, Cabin John began a green competition with neighboring Carderock Springs on which community could collect the most recyclable metals. Cabin John won.

Judy Welles

Reed Martin plays old-time banjo.

A community of independent-minded and creative people, Cabin John is also home to dozens of artists, writers, and musicians. Reed Martin is a well-known banjoist who plays the 5-string banjo in the "old time" or claw hammer style. James Hilleary has been described as a "colorist of formidable ability." Tom Green has exhibited his room-size paintings at the Guggenheim Museum. Constance Bergfors' 9-foot tall wood sculptures now fill a gallery wing of her home as well as the lobby of a major synagogue in Washington, D.C. Photographers, weavers, potters and many others came to Cabin John when housing was affordable and a live-and-let-live attitude encouraged differences.

Cabin John's Divertimento chamber music group.

In 2007, the Cabin John Citizens Association held a contest on what someone moving into Cabin John should know about the community. Among the high points about Cabin John was the statement that "people break into your house to leave stuff."

Also heralded was the annual community summer canoe regatta in which about 30 residents take canoes on the Potomac River, everyone smiling and only a few ending up in the water. Reed Martin's fiberglass bull, which he places at the corner of 79th Street and MacArthur Boulevard to announce community events like the annual house tour, is a standout.

Cabin John was once known only because of a bridge, a hotel and a romantic legend. It was a scenic destination, a place to escape the Nation's Capital's summer heat. The beauty of the area made it a place for development in 1912 as Cabin John Park. Later, holding to rural country ways and close-knit values, residents

Constance Bergfors' graceful, large wood sculptures can be found in the lobby of a synagogue and office buildings in Washington, D.C. and special exhibits.

123

Courtesy Jackie Hoglund

Cabin John canoe "regatta."

compared the community to the L'il Abner cartoon and called it "dogpatch." The area that once did not have the highest reputation has become an increasingly upscale and sought after community close to the river and canal.

The values of small town friendliness, many trees, varied housing, and racial and cultural diversity drew the early residents to Cabin

Tim Weedlun

A fiberglass bull owned by Reed Martin publicizes many community events.

124

John. Those same values were the basis for the 1970 Community Plan. Change is inevitable, and Cabin John is changing house by house. In 2008, residents hope that newcomers will share the community's vision and values. Years from now, what stories will they tell?

Much has changed; much remains the same. Independent-minded people built Cabin John. They lived near, worked on, and loved the river and canal. Many people like them live there today. Just as it was in the past, Cabin John is more than a legend.

Courtesy Richard Cook

Below: Cabin John residents gathered on the Cabin John Bridge to celebrate its reopening after repairs on November 17, 2001. The scene was reminiscent of an earlier time (above) when citizens came together on the bridge in 1865.

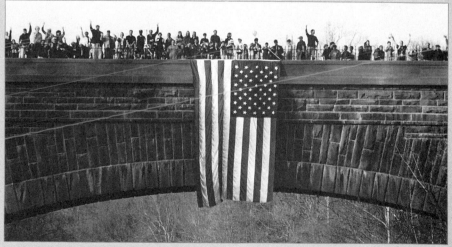

Robert Epstein

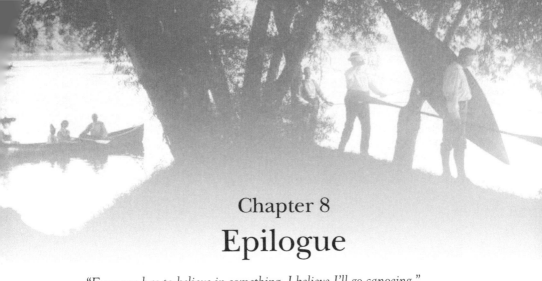

Chapter 8
Epilogue

"Everyone has to believe in something. I believe I'll go canoeing."
—Henry David Thoreau

Kathleen Gates Carroll, a daughter of Chris Gates, lived next to the C&O Canal as a child. She wanted her own daughter to know what life was like for a child in Cabin John in the 1950s and wrote a poem:

Rebecca, my sunny daughter
I wish we had been young together
And you had been there to play with me
By my rocky river.

I'd show you where the purple phlox would bloom
We would pick bunches of them
And take them to
Our Mama/Grandma
And she'd be pleased
And put them around
Our funny house
In mayonnaise jars...

I'd show you
The secret places –
Like the vine that swings out
From the towpath
Almost to the river.
We would swing
And yell like Tarzan
Then splash across the stones
The water drops shimmering
Galaxies of stars.

Then we'd make a huge leap
To the island
Unless we missed
And fell among the water lilies
Where dragonflies would
Buzz around
Mistaking us for their own.

We'd tiptoe around
The poison ivy
Down to the sandbar where
We'd squish our way through the sand
Waves of water
Encircling our feet
Like colossal Atlases
We'd hold up the earth and sky
While minnows sucked our toes...

Or we could catch
Some sun perch
And our cousin Boots would
Fry them up
Crispy fresh
But we wouldn't
Have to eat them
If we didn't want to.

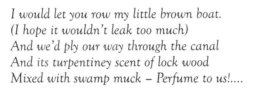

I would let you row my little brown boat.
(I hope it wouldn't leak too much)
And we'd ply our way through the canal
And its turpentiney scent of lock wood
Mixed with swamp muck – Perfume to us!....

And when the purple haze
Would come down the river
And the frogs would croak
And the crickets chirp
We'd hug a long, long hug
And you'd go back to your world
And I to mine.

Taking Canoes on Potomac River, ca. 1900, courtesy Richard Cook.
Drawing by Trudy Nicholson.

Locktenders for the Seven Locks, Chesapeake and Ohio Canal

Lock 8: Solomon Drew, 1830; Levi Barrett, 1839-40; Ayles Stephens, 1850s-70; Elizabeth Davis/John Davis, 1870–1878; Thomas Davis, John H. Morgrel (or Morgrell), 1878-1885; Hamilton Davis, "Old Man" Hamrick, 1900s; Charles Spong, 1915-24.

Locks 9, 10: Thomas Burgess, 1830-35; John Young, 1830s-1840s; John Lambie, 1847; Lucy Metts, 1850s; Marshall and J. W. Burriss, 1870s; Charles Stewart or Steward, 1888; Victor and Vergie Hall, 1915-24; John Swain, Locks 10, 14, 1890-1920.

Lock 11: Mr. Edmonston, 1830.

Locks 12, 13, 14: Charles Sears, 1830; Mr. Ross, 1835; Frederick and Hezekiah Metts, 1839-40; Asa and Rebecca Farmon, 1846; Lawrence and Adelaide Hill, Lock 12, 1860; John Wimmis, Lock 12, 1874; William Davis, John Hamilton, Locks 12, 13, 1915; John "Jack" Speaker, Locks 13, 14, 1900-1924.

Presidents, Cabin John (Park) Citizens Association
(early records incomplete)

1919 -1930s
Andrew C. Wilkins
Charles Godbold
Walter Armstrong
Ellis King
Mr. Hannen

1940s-50s
John Jessup
Annice Tortoro

1960s – 1970s
Victor Niiranen 1967
Donald Herdeck 1968
Judy Toth 1970
Jim Craig 1971
D. Edwin Winslow 1972
Andrew Rice 1975

1980s to Present
Alan van Emmerik 1981
Patrick Connelly 1982
Susan Vogt 1983
Betsy Lawrence 1984
Jack Fellows and Kay Tamzarian 1985
Tevy Schlafman 1986
Maureen Willoughby 1987
Robert Greenburg 1988
Taffy Scott Kingscott 1989-1991
Diane Leatherman 1992
Judy and Fred Mopsik 1993
Harry and Lori Rieckelman 1995
Burr Gray 1996 -

Fire Chiefs, Cabin John Park Volunteer Fire Department

1930-31	Norman Lynch
1930	Graham Sullivan
1933	Hubert Streams
1934-37	C. Kipps
1937	J. Johnson
1938	W. Curtain
1939	Norman Hunt
1940-41	Kenneth Tuohey
1942	Norman Hunt
1943-46	D. Tuohey
1947-50	Otie M. Howell
1951	Kenneth Tuohey
1952	Ed Kerns
1953	Otie M. Howell
1954-61	Donald Marshall
1961-62	Frank Prather
1962-64	G. Tuohey
1964	R. W. Hook; G. Tuohey
1965	Frank N. Prather, Sr.
1966	R. W. Hook
1967	G. Tuohey
1968-72	Frank N. Prather, Sr.
1973-74	E. C. Gotthardt, Sr.
1975	D. G. Power, Sr.
1976-85	D. A. Money
1986-91	V. H. Esch, Jr.
1992 to present	James P. Seavey, Sr.

Editors of *The Village News* (1967 - 2008)

Csanad Toth
Susan Vogt
Mary Anne Wilson
Shelly Keller
Minda Wetzel
Bobbi Stuart
Betsy Cheney and Alan Bookman
Linda Billings, Cappie Morgan
Kathy Orme
Andrew Rice
Lauren Forestall
Gerald Quinn
Heidi Brown Lewis
Mike Miller and Tim Weedlun

Bibliography

...erson, Carlotta. Glen Echo: The Remarkable Saga of a Very Small ...n. Town of Glen Echo, 2006.

...trong, Edith Martin, Brief History of Cabin John Park, 1947.

...rong, Edith Martin, Days at Cabin John, Vantage Press, 1958.

...gen, Willis, "Cabin John and the Bobingers," The Montgomery County Story, Vol. VII, No. 4, Montgomery County Historical Society, August 1964.

Cabin John Park Citizens Association, Constitution & By-Laws, July 1928 (courtesy Reed Martin).

Cabin John Land Development Corp. Tract Map (courtesy Barbara Martin).

Clara Barton Elementary School PTA Executive Committee, "Integrated Program at Clara Barton Elementary School," Report of the School Relations Committee, April 19, 1958.

Cohen, Roger S., Jr., "Glen Echo-Cabin John Area of Montgomery County, Maryland," The Montgomery County Story, Vol. VII, No. 4, Montgomery County Historical Society, August 1964.

Coldham, Peter Wilson, Settlers of Maryland 1679-1700; 1701-1730, Genealogical Publishing Co., 1995.

Cook, Eleanor M. V., "History of Early Water Mills in Montgomery County, Maryland," Montgomery County Historical Society, 1990.

Crook, Mary Charlotte, "The David W. Taylor Naval Ship Research and Development Center," The Montgomery County Story, Vol. 22, No. 3, Montgomery County Historical Society, August 1979.

Dwyer, Michael, Images of America: Montgomery County, Arcadia Publishing, 2006.

Federal Writers Project (WPA), Washington City & Capital, Washington, D.C., 1937.

Fitzsimons, Mrs. Neal, "Building of the Cabin John Bridge," The Montgomery County Story, Vol. XVI, No. 1, Montgomery County Historical Society, February 1973.

Fitzsimons, Mrs. Neal, "Gold Mines of Montgomery County," The Montgomery County Story, Vol. XV, No. 3, Montgomery County Historical Society, May 1972.

Fogle, David, professor and six students of University of Maryland School of Architecture, "Cabin John Mail-Order Homes Historic District Study," 1987.

Fradin, Morris, Hey-ey-ey, Lock! Adventure on the Chesapeake & Ohio Canal, See-And-Know Press, Cabin John, Md., 1974.

Gaillard, D. D., "Washington Aqueduct and Cabin John Bridge," National Geographic Magazine, Vol. VIII, No. 12, December 1897.

Hahn, Thomas F., Towpath Guide to the Chesapeake & Ohio Canal: Georgetown Tidelock to Cumberland, American Canal and Transportation Center, 1994.

Harris, Ann Paterson, Potomac Adventure: Pre-History to Present, Jantron, 1978.

Hopkins, G. M., Atlas of Fifteen Miles Around Washington including Montgomery County Maryland, Stearn Lithographic Press, 1879.

Johnson, Charles T., Jr., Legend of the Female Stranger: A Tale of Cabin John Bridge and Old Alexandria, Press of Wm. T. Hynes, Baltimore, 1912.

Kytle, Elizabeth, Home On the Canal, Johns Hopkins University Press, 1983.

Kytle, Elizabeth, Time Was: A Cabin John Memory Book, Interviews with 18 Old-Timers, Cabin John Citizens Association, 1976.

Marriott., J. H. Wilson, Picturesque Cabin John: A Bit of History, 1903.

Offutt, William, Bethesda: A Social History of the Area Through World War Two, Innovation Game, 1996.

Restoration of Name of Jefferson Davis to Cabin John Bridge, Official Correspondence, Confederated Southern Memorial Association of New Orleans, 1909.

Story of Cabin John, presentations at PTA meeting, transcript, December 3, 1957.

Sween, Jane C., and William Offutt, Montgomery County: Centuries of Change, American Historical Press, 1999.

Kilp, Frederick, This Was Potomac River, self-published, 1978.

Tomlinson, J. S., "Cabin John Park, A Picture and Paragraph Story," 1913.

Tomlinson, J. S., "Cabin John Park, Section One," American Land Co., 1914.

Tomlinson, J. S., "Cabin John Park, Section Four," American Land Co., 1914.

Tomlinson, J. S., "Cabin John Park, Section 4, Along the Potomac Highlands," American Land Co., 1913.

Thompson, Toby, "In Heaven There Is No Beer...But Heaven's Not Cabin John," Washington Post, May 18, 1969.

The Village News, 1967-2007.

The Washington Post Archives

The Washington Star Archives

Ways, Harry C., History of the Washington Aqueduct, 1994.

Illustrations

Front cover
Photographer Alex J. Yowell's studio under the Cabin John Bridge, ca. 1900.

Foreword
Page v   Cabin John Creek.
Page vii   Canoeing on the Potomac River, ca. 1900.

Chapter 1. The Legends
Page 2   Gravestone of the Female Stranger.
Page 3   Book cover, Legend of the Female Stranger, 1912.
Page 4   Drawing of the hermit's cabin, 1903.
Page 5   Cabin under the Union Arch Bridge, ca. 1880.
Page 7   Map of Captain John Smith's journey on Chesapeake Bay and Potomac River in 1608.

Chapter 2. River, Canal, and Roads
Page 10   1878 map by G. M. Hopkins.
Page 11   Birdie Hook, 1920.
Page 12   1936 Potomac River flood at Lockhouse 8.
Page 12   Flood damage at Lock 8.
Page 13   C&O Canal payboat going through Lock 8 in 1910.
Page 14   Lockhouse 8 in 1938.
Page 14   Lock 9 "waithouse" and Lockhouse 10 in 1913.
Page 15   Lockhouse 9, ca. 1939.
Page 15   Lockhouse 10 in 2008.
Page 16   Walking on towpath.
Page 17   Conduit Road in 1912.
Page 17   MacArthur Boulevard truck weight limit sign.
Page 20   Cabin John Parkway under Union Arch Bridge.
Page 21   Clara Barton Parkway exit to Cabin John.

Chapter 3. Rural to Residential
Page 23   Cabin John farmland, 1912.
Page 24   Thomas Tuohey's house in 1913.
Page 24   Tuohey house in 2007.
Page 26   Map of Tract 1, Cabin John Park.
Page 27   Cabin John Park advertisement "3 Dozen Attractive Features."
Page 28   Map of Tract 2, Cabin John Park.
Page 29   Map of Tract 4, Cabin John Park.
Page 30   David Tuohey's house, owned by Barbara and Reed Martin, 2008.
Page 32   Sears kit house ("Hampton" model) built by Sullivan family, 1925.
Page 34   Sullivan family's other Sears kit house, 1920.
Page 34   Sullivan family's 1920 Sears kit house restored by Hornauer family.
Page 35   Jenny Sullivan's Great Falls pop stand.
Page 35   Granny Sullivan and family members.

Page 36   Worsham/Cable family Sears kit house.
Page 36   Children across from Marshall home.
Page 36   Gates sisters swimming in canal.
Page 36   Gates family house on canal, ca. 1940.
Page 37   Chris Gates with canal pleasure boat, 1940s.
Page 37   Rammed earth house.
Page 38   Log house.
Page 39   Villa house.
Page 39   Modern house.
Page 40   Tommy and Naomi Denell, 2007.
Page 40   Dome house.
Page 41   New house, 2007.
Page 42   Cabin John Gardens, early 1940s.
Page 45   Carver Road, 1940s.
Page 46   Organizers of first Crab Feast, 1970.
Page 49   Cabin John Creek, 2008.
Page 50   MacArthur Park.
Page 51   MacArthur House condominium apartment building.

Chapter 4. Union Arch Bridge

Page 52   Capt. Montgomery C. Meigs.
Page 53   Bridge No. 3, 2007.
Page 53   Bridge No. 3, 1913.
Page 54   Walking on Bridge No. 3.
Page 55   Wooden trestle support for center arch of Union Arch Bridge.
Page 56   Civil War wagons on bridge.
Page 57   Bridge without Jefferson Davis name.
Page 57   J. B. Horne restores Jefferson Davis name.
Page 58   J. B. Horne with his tools.
Page 59   Wooden stairs to Cabin John Creek, ca. 1900.
Page 59   Bicyclists at bridge, 1883.
Page 60   Frozen leaks from bridge conduit, 1910.
Page 61   Trucks and children on bridge in 1940s.
Page 62   Cabin John T-shirt with bridge design.
Page 62   Traffic at bridge, 2007.
Page 63   Broken ledge on bridge, 1974.

Chapter 5. Cabin John Bridge Hotel

Page 65   Rosa Bobinger.
Page 66   Front of Cabin John Bridge Hotel.
Page 67   Bowl from Cabin John Bridge Hotel.
Page 67   Bobinger gravesite.
Page 68   Cabin John Bridge with hotel in distance, ca. 1902.
Page 69   Fanciful illustration of hotel.
Page 69   Lovers Lane Bridge from hotel over canal to towpath.
Page 70   Gazebo summer house.

Page 70   Hotel dining room.
Page 71   Ornate gazebo near hotel orchestrion, 1900.
Page 71   Rear of hotel with orchestrion.
Page 72   Hotel dinner bill.
Page 72   Hotel carriage house, ca. 1910.
Page 73   1930 trolley.
Page 74   Iron bridge to hotel, ca. 1900.
Page 75   Early 1900s advertisement "Favorite Resort of the Washington Public."
Page 77   Dick Mansfield cartoon about Cabin John Bridge Hotel for *The Washington Post*, 1947.
Page 78   Hotel gas house.

Chapter 6. A Community Grows

Page 80   Junior Hall, 2007.
Page 82   *The Village News* redesigned.
Page 83   Cabin John Park Volunteer Fire Department volunteers, 1933.
Page 83   1935 Brockway fire truck.
Page 84   Cabin John Park Volunteer Fire Department firehouse, 1973.
Page 85   Firehose hookup trophy.
Page 86   Fire truck mailbox.
Page 86   Mary Hook Morgal and firehorn trophy.
Page 87   Cabin John majorettes, "The CJs," ca. 1960.
Page 88   Converted firehouse.
Page 88   Cabin John Park Volunteer Fire Department firehouse, 2008.
Page 89   River rescue, 1973.
Page 90   Danny Harris.
Page 92   Moses Hall exhibit panel dedication, 2007.
Page 92   Hermon Church.
Page 93   G. W. Shaler Memorial Methodist Episcopal Church bell from 1926.
Page 93   Cabin John United Methodist Church.
Page 94   St. George Coptic Orthodox Church.
Page 95   Friendship School.
Page 96   Cabin John-Glen Echo sign.
Page 97   Theodore Denell 7th grade report card, 1913.
Page 97   Glen Echo-Cabin John School, ca. 1928.
Page 99   Tennis courts and hotel gas house.
Page 100   Glen Echo-Cabin John School segregated class, 1954.
Page 100   Glen Echo-Cabin John School integrated class, 1955.
Page 101   Clara Barton School Community Center.
Page 102   Cabin John Post Office, 1913, later Tuohey's Tavern.
Page 102   U. S. Post Office in Cabin John, 2008.
Page 104   Cabin John Mills, possibly 1850s.
Page 105   Alpine Veterinarian Hospital, site of Judge Benson's store.
Page 107   Captain's Market (a.k.a. Good and Quick).

ge 107 Group at Tuohey's Tavern.
age 108 Tearing down Tuohey's Tavern.
Page 108 MacArthur Plaza shopping center.
Page 109 Bethesda Co-Op natural food market.
Page 110 Corner of MacArthur Boulevard and Seven Locks Road.
Page 111 Level Fitness, formerly site of Dorothy Helen's beauty parlor.
Page 111 Program cover from 1976 Chautauqua celebration.

Chapter 7. A Way of Life

Page 113 Cabin John canoe "regatta" in Potomac River, 2007.
Page 114 Young Doug Cable fished at edge of Potomac River, 1950s.
Page 115 Cable/Swisher/Fyock family, 2007.
Page 115 Lew Worsham, golfer.
Page 116 Lockhouse 8 and neighboring houses, 1938.
Page 117 Lillian "Blyzz" Fields with friends at Lockhouse 8, 1940.
Page 117 Lockkeeper's grandson, Jack Fields, at Lockhouse 8, 1940.
Page 118 Gravesite of last Lock 8 locktender, Charles Spong.
Page 118 Myrtle Spong Muck at Lockhouse 8, 1940s.
Page 120 Teens at Good & Quick counter.
Page 122 Reed Martin plays old-time banjo.
Page 123 Divertimento chamber music group.
Page 123 Constance Bergfors' large wood sculpture.
Page 124 Cabin John canoe "regatta."
Page 124 Fiberglass bull.
Page 125 Union Arch bridge celebration, 1865.
Page 125 Cabin John Bridge reopening celebration in 2001.

Chapter 8. Epilogue

Page 126 Taking canoes on the Potomac River, ca. 1900.

Back cover

Book cover, Legend of the Female Stranger, 1912.
Cabin John canoe "regatta" on Potomac River, 2007.
Cabin John Gardens, early 1940s.
Cabin John majorettes, "The CJs," ca. 1960.
Postcard of photographer Alex J. Yowell's studio under the bridge, 1915.

Index

A

African Americans, viii, ix, 16, 25, 32, 33, 41, 44, 45, 51, 91, 92, 99, 100, 111
American Land Co., ix, 4, 23, 24, 27, 30, 32
Amusement parks, 11, 19, 76, 120
Aqueduct, see Washington Aqueduct
Architects, 38, 39, 42
Armstrong, David, 81
Armstrong, Edith, vi, 4, 5, 9, 19, 111
Armstrong, Walter B., 79, 129

B

Baptist, LaVerne, 103
Barber, Marvin, 90
Barton, Clara, 98
Beall, Thomas, 23
Behan, Katie Walker, 58
Bell, Joan, 90
Bell, Ray, 90
Beltway, 9, 20, 46
Benson, Charles, 24, 31, 82, 93
Bergfors, Constance, 122
Bethesda Co-op, x, 109
Billings, Linda, 81, 82
Blacks, see African Americans
Blacksmiths, 31, 33, 82, 105
Bobinger, George, 68
Bobinger, Harry, 76
Bobinger, Mrs. Harry (Mildred), 112
Bobinger, Joseph, 23-25, 56, 65-68, 72, 73, 102
Bobinger, Mary, 41, 76, 97
Bobinger, Rosa, 65-68, 73
Bobinger, William, 41, 68, 76
Bridges, 53, 54, 69, 74, 89, 105, 119. See also Union Arch Bridge
Brown, David, 39
Brown, Henry, 25
Brown, Lena, 25

C

Cabin John Bridge, see Union Arch Bridge
Cabin John Bridge Hotel, v, viii, ix, 3, 11, 19, 25, 41, 42, 65-78, 85, 97, 99, 102, 112, 120, 122
Cabin John Citizens Association, ix, 3, 32, 33, 43, 45-48, 62-64, 79-82, 91-106 passim, 121-123
Cabin John Creek, 1, 6-28 passim, 41-74 passim, 81, 91, 103
Cabin John Gardens, ix, 31, 41-44, 106-114 passim, 121
Cabin John Gardens Citizens Association, 43
Cabin John Mills, 8, 9, 103, 104
Cabin John Park, 23-34 passim, 79, 93, 106, 113, 124
Cabin John Park Citizens Association, see Cabin John Citizens Association
Cabin John Park Volunteer Fire Department, 25, 32, 33, 39, 82-89, 108, 121, 122
Cabin John Parkway, 20, 53, 63
Cable, Uva, and family, vi, 36, 113-115
Canal, see Chesapeake and Ohio Canal
Cannon, Joe, 72
Captain John's Creek/Run, see Cabin John Creek
Carper, Irene, 102
Carper, Wilbur, 102
Carroll, Kathleen Gates, vi, 35, 126
Carver Road, ix, 25, 41, 44-46
Case, William, 106
Cemeteries and graves, 2, 3, 13, 52, 67, 91-93, 117, 118
Cerniglia, Christine Gates, vi, 35
Chandler, Rev. Dennis, 121
Chautauqua, 110, 111
Chesapeake and Ohio Canal, vi, viii-x, 9-44 passim, 54-56, 68-70, 84, 89, 94, 96, 104, 105, 112-128 passim
Chesapeake and Ohio Canal National Historical Park, v, x, 90
Churches, 6, 45, 92, 94, 96, 114. See also names of specific churches

Citizen associations, see:
  Cabin John Citizens Association
  Cabin John Gardens Citizens
    Association
Civil defense, 85, 90, 121
Civil War, viii, 18, 23, 34, 42, 55, 56, 58, 64, 67
Civilian Conservation Corps, 12, 89
Clara Barton Parkway, x, 19-21, 46, 115, 117, 118
Clara Barton School, ix, 81, 98-101, 103, 112
Clark, Dottie, 87
Cleveland, Grover, 18
Community Plan, x, 46-50, 125
Conduit Road, 11, 16-18, 25-41 passim, 60, 66, 68, 82-106 passim. See also MacArthur Boulevard
Cook, Richard, vi, 29, 62, 76
Corps of Engineers, U.S., 16, 17, 52-64 passim
Crab Feast, x, 46, 81, 122
Crook, Jesse, 30, 31

D

David Taylor Model Basin, ix, 25, 41, 42, 45, 90, 113
Davis, Jefferson, viii, ix, 56-58, 67
Denell, Naomi, vi, 40, 121
Denell, Tommy, vi, 40, 97, 106, 107
Dentzel, Gustav, 76
Dodge, Charles, 94
Dolezal, Vera, 112
Douglas, William O., ix, 15
Downzoning, see Community Plan
Dowling family, 23-25, 27, 93, 94
Drew, Solomon, 115
Duncan, Rev. G. S., 93

F

Female stranger, 2, 3
Fields, Jack, 111, 117
Fields, John, 116, 118
Fields, Myrtle Spong, 116-118
Fire department, see Cabin John Park Volunteer Fire Department
Firehouses, ix, 11, 33, 47, 82-88 passim, 105

Fleete, Henry, 22
Fletchall, Capt. Thomas, 23
Floods, ix, 11, 12, 15, 118-120
Four Horsemen, 79
Fradin, Morris, 109, 111
Friendship School, viii, 29, 95
Fyock family, vi, 43, 113-115

G

Gates family, vi, 35-37, 116, 126
Gibson Grove church, ix, 45, 91, 99
Gibson, Sarah, 91
Glen Echo, 13, 19, 22, 64, 76, 84, 96-110 passim, 119, 120
Glen Echo-Cabin John School, ix, 95-100 passim
Godbold, Charles H., 79
Godbold, Josephine, 79
Gold, 18, 30, 74
Goodman, Charles, 39
Great Falls, 9, 13, 16-20, 34, 35, 53, 60, 61, 90, 106
Green, Tom, 122
Griffith, Edward, 23
Gude, Gilbert, 64
Gulley Guards, 121

H

Hall, Victor, 116
Hall, Virgie, 116
Harris, Danny, 90, 91
Havens, Josephine, 18, 25
Helen, Dorothy, 109, 111
Heflin, Larry, 11
Hermon church, viii, 67, 68, 92-94, 121
Hilleary, James, 122
Home Demonstration Club, ix, 80
Home Study, 45
Hook, Birdie, 11
Hornauer, Elaine, vi, 34
Horne, J. B., 57, 58
Hotel, see Cabin John Bridge Hotel
Humphrey, Harry, 37
Humphrey, Hubert, v, 38
Humphrey, Olive, 37
Hutton, William R., 56

I

Iglehart, Mrs. Don, 47
Indians, see Native Americans
Irish laborers, vi, 13, 25, 94, 113

J

Jessup, John, 47
Jewell, E. Guy, 95, 96
John of the Cabin, 1-6, 104
Junior Hall, 80

K

Kepler, Ritch, 109
King, Ellis R., 79
Kytle, Calvin, 109
Kytle, Elizabeth, vi, 47, 93, 110

L

Ladies Auxiliary, 85, 86, 121
Lawrence, Charlie, 87
Lawrence, Margaret, 87
Leatherman, Diane, 46, 91
Lehr, Bill, 120
Lincoln, Abraham, 18, 56
Lockhouses, 11-15, 35, 36, 40, 89, 115-120
Locktenders, vi, viii, 13, 14, 40, 113-120 passim, 128
Loeb, Ellen, 112
Lupton, Dana Swisher, vi, 43, 106, 115

M

MacArthur Boulevard, 16, 17, 19, 31, 41, 53, 54, 81, 82, 87, 91, 96, 105, 110, 121, 123. See also Conduit Road
MacArthur Plaza, x, 36, 50, 80, 102, 108, 109
Magruder, Patrick, 103, 104
Majorettes, 87, 121
Manion, Tom, 39
Marshall, Pearman, 91
Marshall, Thelma, 44
Martin, Barbara, vi, 31, 45, 82
Martin, Reed, vi, 30, 35, 122-124
Mater, Evan, vi, 41

McCann, John, 119
McIntyre, Robert, 57
McKelvey, Laura, 103
McKinney, Frank, 45, 46
Meigs, Capt. Montgomery C., 5, 52-55, 58
Methodist church, ix, 33, 93, 94, 102-110 passim, 117, 118, 121
Mills, 1, 8, 9, 103, 104. See also Cabin John Mills
Model Basin, see David Taylor Model Basin
Moore, Capt. John, 6, 16, 25, 94
Moore's School, viii, 99
Morgal, D. Everett, 86
Morgal, Mary Hook, vi, 11, 86-87, 90, 120
Morgal, Ralph, 91
Moses Hall, 91, 92, 99
Muck, Charles, 118
Murphy, David, vi, 122
Murphy, Olivia, vi, 122
Myers, Billie, 121
Myers, Eva Dell, 119

N

Native Americans, viii, 1, 6, 9, 16, 22, 54, 112
Naval Surface Warfare Center, see David Taylor Model Basin
Neudorfer, Bill, 39
New Lost City Ramblers, 109
Newman, Dagny, 43, 44

O

O'Brien, James, 12
Offutt, James, 103
Offutt, William, 16, 55, 61, 67, 68, 90, 119, 120
Olson, Louise, 112

P

Palisades Pool, 46
Palm Garden, 76, 77
Patch, Robert, 109
Persimmon Tree Road, viii, 16, 19, 25, 29, 31, 33, 53, 77, 94, 110, 121
Peter, Robert, 23

eyton, Frances, 114
Pirates, 1, 3-6, 30
Plummers Island, 11, 15
Population, 33, 41, 47, 48, 51, 53, 67,
  88, 97, 102, 113
Post office, x, 19, 31, 50, 102, 103, 106,
  108
Potomac River, v, vii-ix, 2, 6-13, 19-29
  passim, 38, 43, 48, 52, 53, 61, 65-76
  passim, 81, 89, 114, 119-125
Potter, Alden A., 85
Potter, Buzzy, 119
Potter, Neal, v, 85, 96, 98

Q

Quarantine, 60
Quarries, 6, 16, 41, 55, 89, 104, 105
Quinn, Gerald, vi, 39

R

Rabner, John, 109
Railways and trolleys, 15, 19, 25, 31, 32,
  73-76, 110
Read, John, 23
Reading, William, 66, 94
Redden, Isabelle, 31, 114
Redden, Percy, 31, 114
Rice, Andrew, vi, 22, 48, 51, 82, 98, 109,
  112
Rieke, Rev. Allyn, 64
River rats, 120, 121
River Road, 1, 16, 17, 88, 89, 99, 103,
  105
Rives, Alfred L., 54
Roads and highways, see names of
  specific roads
Roark, Mike, 109
Roberts, Susan, 51
Roosevelt, Eleanor, 90
Roosevelt, Franklin, 81, 89
Roosevelt, Theodore, 18, 58, 72
Rose, Lena, 46

S

Saunders, John, 94
Schools, viii, ix, 21, 31, 40, 45, 80, 81,
  91-102 passim, 111. See also names of
  specific schools

Scott, Charles, 102
Scott, Clarabell, 42
Scott, Clarence, 42
Sears houses, v, 32-36, 41, 114
Seven locks, viii, 11, 13, 117
Seven Locks Road, 16, 51
Shaler, G. W., 93
Shaw, Jerry, 77
Shuff, Charlie, 105
Shuff, Joan, 36
Shuff, Ruth Tuohey, 103, 105
Shuler, Shirley, 103
Smith, Caleb B., 56
Smith, Charles, 31, 80
Smith, Mrs. Charles, 96
Smith, Capt. John, viii, x, 6-9, 22
Smith, Roy C., 5
Soda fountain, 106, 107
Sousa, John Philip, v, 74
Spates, Walt, 106
Spong family, 116-118, 120
Springmann, Ralph, 20, 33, 93
Squatters, 15, 119
Stein, Margaret, 101
Stephens, Lillian Fields, 11, 116-118
Stores, 25, 31, 32, 82, 89, 96, 102-109
  passim, 120, 121. See also MacArthur
  Plaza
Sullivan family, vi, 32-35, 42, 50
Swainson, William E., 119, 120
Swedenburg, Celeste, 45, 46
Swisher, Wayne, and family, vi, 43, 91,
  106, 113-115, 121

T

Taft, William Howard, 72
Tomlinson, J. S., 23-31 passim, 53, 97
Thompson, Betty, 39
Thompson, Charley, 39
Thompson, John, 23
Thompson, Mary, 23
Thompson, Toby, 107
Tuohey, David, 30, 33, 83, 85, 98, 106,
  108
Tuohey, Dennis, 25, 32, 85, 102, 103
Tuohey, Gordon, 84
Tuohey, Kenneth, 86
Tuohey, Loretta, 11, 82, 84
Tuohey, Mary O'Brien, 30, 31
Tuohey, Norman, 25, 32, 74, 95, 104

Tuohey, Pat, 36
Tuohey, Thomas, 11, 23-25
Tuohey's Tavern, 25, 30, 31, 35, 85, 102,
    106-108, 120
Trolleys, see Railways and trolleys

U

Union Arch Bridge, v, viii-x, 1, 3, 5, 8,
    11, 16-32 passim, 52-68, 73-78, 82,
    84, 96, 97, 101, 123, 125

V

Veterans of Foreign Wars, 90, 91
Village News, The, vi, x, 22, 45, 62, 81,
    82, 98, 109, 111
Vogt, Peter, 46

W

Washington Aqueduct, v, viii, 1, 5, 16,
    17, 34, 52-67 passim, 84, 85, 88, 105,
    121
Ways, Harry, 63
Wedding, James H., 90
Wedding, Presley, 61
Weil, George L., v, 38
Wetzel, Minda, 64
White, Bill, 45, 46
White, Hugh, 105
White, Joseph, 23
Widmayer, Jack, 42
Widmayer, Lincoln, 42
Wilkins, A. C., 79
Wilkoff, Bob, 39
Williams, Garland, 118
Williams, Jimmy, 105
Williams, Susan, 118
Willoughby, Maureen, vi, 121
Wilner, Jim, 39
Wilson Lane, 19, 31, 95-98
Wilson, Woodrow, 72
Winslow, D. Edwin, 48
Wood, Rocky, 38
Worsham family, 36, 87, 90, 113-115
World War II, 16, 41, 43, 77, 84, 85, 89,
    90

Tim Shank

About the Author

Judith Welles, a writer, columnist, and blogger, lives in Cabin John. With a career in journalism and public relations for government and industry, she currently writes about work life and local history for magazines in Maryland and the Washington, D.C. metropolitan area. She also managed restoration of a canal lockhouse for the Potomac Conservancy and National Park Service and developed visitor programs on the history, culture and ecology of the C&O Canal and Potomac River. Judy is married to Tim Shank and has two sons and a step-daughter.

Back Cover: Book, Legend of the Female Stranger, 1912, courtesy Richard Cook; Cabin John canoe "regatta" on Potomac River, 2007, Katherine T. Andrle; Cabin John Gardens, early 1940s, MNCPPC; Cabin John majorettes, "The CJs," ca. 1960, courtesy Mary Morgal; postcard of photographer Alex J. Yowell's studio, ca. 1915, courtesy Richard Cook.